# *Show Up More Emotionally*

*A Simple Guide to Reconnecting With Your Emotions and Yourself*

**Jim Sabellico**

ONE

---

# *Introduction*

Most people spend their lives trying to hold it together.

You learn early that emotions make things complicated, so you get good at managing them. You learn to keep calm, stay steady, and move on quickly. And for a while, that works. You become the reliable one. The strong one. The person everyone can count on.

But somewhere along the way, strength starts to feel heavy.

You go through your days doing everything right. Working hard, showing up, keeping peace, and yet something inside still feels off. You tell yourself you should be fine, that other people have it worse, that there's no reason to feel this way. But late at night, when the world gets quiet, you can feel the truth pressing through the calm. You're tired. Not the kind of tired that sleep fixes, but the kind that lives deep inside.

You've been strong for so long that you forgot what safe feels like.

That's what emotional exhaustion really is. It's not weakness or failure; it's the natural result of living disconnected from what you feel. You've spent years containing, controlling, or minimizing your emotions so life could keep moving. You've gotten so used to surviving that you stopped noticing what it costs to stay that composed.

It shows up in ways that are easy to overlook. The short temper you can't explain. The restlessness that follows you even when you're "relaxing." The numbness that creeps in where excitement used to live. You might still be performing calm, but inside, something is straining under the weight of all that unexpressed life.

If you've ever thought, "I should be happy, but I just don't feel it," you're not alone. You're not broken. You're just full. Full of years of emotions that never got their chance to be felt.

We live in a world that teaches us to prioritize productivity over presence. We measure success by what we can control, not by how connected we feel. We praise emotional restraint, not emotional understanding. But eventually, that approach stops working. You can only outrun your feelings for so long before your body and mind start asking for your attention.

This book is not about becoming more emotional. It's about becoming more whole. It's about learning to listen to what your emotions have been trying to tell you instead of constantly trying to manage them. It's about turning toward the parts of you you've ignored for years. Not to fall apart, but to finally feel at peace.

You don't need to learn how to be strong. You already know that. You need to learn how to feel safe enough to stop performing strength all the time.

Over the next few chapters, we'll explore how emotional disconnection happens, what it costs, and how to begin feeling again in a way that's grounded, not chaotic. You'll learn how to recognize the signs of survival mode, understand the emotions that live underneath it, and begin rebuilding trust with yourself.

This is not a book about fixing your emotions. It's about understanding them. It's about giving language to what has felt confusing and permission to what has felt off-limits. It's about remembering that your emotions were never the problem. They were the proof that you cared, the evidence that you were still alive, and the compass guiding you back home.

So if you've been holding it all together for a little too long, take a breath. You don't have to keep pretending that fine is enough. You don't have to keep carrying what you've outgrown.

You can show up fully. Not as the version of you that's perfectly composed, but as the one who's finally ready to feel.

Because you don't fall apart when you feel. You fall apart when you stop.

TWO

---

# *Always Fine, Never Okay*

There are two words most people say more than any others when they are trying to keep it together. "I'm fine."

You say it when you are tired but don't want to explain. You say it when someone asks how you are, and you know they don't really want the truth. You say it when you are overwhelmed but determined to look composed. You say it until it becomes a reflex, a mask you put on before you even realize it is there.

For a while, "I'm fine" seems harmless. It keeps the peace. It keeps conversations short. It keeps people from worrying. It also keeps you from being seen.

When you spend years being fine, you begin to confuse it with being okay. But fine is not peace. Fine is the pause button on honesty. Fine is what you say when you have lost touch with what you really feel. It is emotional autopilot. You are moving, speaking, smiling, but not connecting to what is happening inside.

Many people grow up learning that fine is the safest answer. Maybe you learned it from parents who were too busy to handle big feelings. Maybe you learned it from teachers who valued obedience over authenticity. Maybe you learned it from relationships where your emotions were dismissed or minimized. Over time, fine became your language for survival.

It works, until it doesn't.

Eventually, something inside you begins to ache. You can feel it when you're quiet, that low hum of emptiness that sits behind your calm. You catch yourself wondering why you don't feel joy the way you used to, why you can't relax even when you have the chance, why every emotion feels dulled or delayed. That's what happens when you've been fine for too long. You start to lose your sense of aliveness.

Being fine is not the same as being numb. It's more like being muted. Life still moves, but the sound is softer, the colors less vivid. You go through the motions, but it feels like watching someone else's life play out. You check the boxes, you do what is expected, but nothing lands the way it should.

You might notice it most in quiet moments. The drive home after a long day. The pause before bed when you finally put your phone down. The stillness makes space for the truth to rise, and you can feel it — that pull inside you that says, "I'm not actually fine." But before you can even think it through, the habit kicks in. You push the feeling away. You scroll, you work, you distract. Anything to keep the calm intact.

It is easy to judge yourself for this, to wonder why you can't just feel freely or be more open. But this pattern isn't weakness. It is protection. Somewhere in your life, being emotional stopped feeling safe. Maybe you were told to toughen up. Maybe your feelings made someone else uncomfortable. Maybe you learned that your calmness kept everyone else stable. Whatever the reason, your system adapted. It decided that fine was safer than honest.

And in fairness, it worked for a long time. It allowed you to navigate chaos, maintain control, and appear strong. But what kept you safe then is now keeping you stuck. The version of you that can handle everything has no room to feel anything. You can't heal in the same environment where you learned to hide.

The moment you stop hiding behind "I'm fine" is the moment you start coming back to life. It begins with small acts of honesty. When someone asks how you are, you can still say you're okay, but let yourself pause for half a second longer before you answer. Notice what is actually true underneath. Maybe you're tired. Maybe you're sad. Maybe you're just disconnected. Whatever it is, acknowledge it, even if you only whisper it to yourself. That small acknowledgment is where reconnection begins.

At first, honesty feels awkward. It might even feel dangerous. You've built a life around being steady, and honesty introduces uncertainty. What if people don't understand? What if it makes things messy? The reality is, authenticity always feels uncomfortable to someone who has lived behind a mask. The discomfort is not danger. It is evidence that you are stepping into something new.

The habit of fine runs deep. It won't unravel overnight. You will catch yourself saying it out of reflex, smiling when you want to cry, staying quiet when you want to speak. That is okay. Every time you notice the pattern, you weaken it. Every time you choose to be honest, even in a small way, you make space for something real.

In time, you will begin to realize that honesty does not break relationships; it strengthens them. Vulnerability does not make you weak; it makes you human. Feeling does not mean losing control; it means reclaiming connection. The goal is not to stop being composed. The goal is to let composure come from truth instead of suppression.

You don't have to stop saying you're fine. You just have to stop believing that fine is the goal. Fine was the way you survived. It's not the way you heal.

Real peace doesn't come from holding it together. It comes from learning to be honest enough to say, "I'm not fine right now, but I'm here. And that's a start."

THREE

---

# *The Cost of Control*

Control often begins as a good thing. It helps you organize your world, anticipate problems, and protect yourself from chaos. It keeps things running smoothly and gives you the illusion of safety. You can plan, predict, and prepare. But somewhere along the way, control stops being a tool and starts becoming a shield.

Most people who struggle with control do not realize they are doing it out of fear. It doesn't feel like fear. It feels like responsibility. It feels like competence. It feels like strength. You tell yourself that someone has to hold everything together, that if you just stay focused and disciplined, nothing will fall apart. And because you are good at it, people trust you to keep things steady. That trust feels validating at first. Eventually, it becomes pressure.

You start to believe that if you stop paying attention, everything will collapse. Rest becomes guilt. Delegation feels impossible. Spontaneity feels reckless. You learn to equate control with peace, but control isn't peace. It's management. It's the constant effort to keep uncertainty at bay. And the harder you work to manage everything, the more anxious you become when something slips outside your reach.

The truth is that control is born from a lack of safety. At some point, life taught you that unpredictability meant pain. Maybe it was growing up in a home where moods shifted without warning. Maybe it was being let down by people you needed to rely on. Maybe it was one big loss that made you decide that certainty was the only way to protect yourself from being hurt again. Whatever the cause, control became the way you survived.

You learned how to read situations quickly, how to anticipate needs, how to calm other people before they even realized they were upset. You became the one who smoothed things over, the one who could keep chaos contained. It felt like power, but it was actually vigilance. You weren't thriving; you were constantly scanning.

Over time, control begins to take things from you. It takes your rest, because your mind never stops running. It takes your joy, because joy requires surrender. It takes your creativity, because creativity lives in uncertainty. It takes your relationships, because people can feel when you are holding on too tightly. The very thing that helped you survive becomes the thing that isolates you.

Control gives you the illusion of strength, but underneath it lives fear. The fear of disappointment, of being misunderstood, of being vulnerable, of losing stability. You might not call it fear, but you feel it every time you double-check something you've already done, every time you can't relax until everything is perfect, every time you replay a conversation in your head, hoping you said the right thing.

What makes control so seductive is that it works—until it doesn't. It lets you avoid feeling helpless, but it also keeps you from experiencing true connection. You can't be fully present with people if you are always managing how things will go. You can't feel real peace if you are always preparing for what might go wrong. You can't feel safe if safety depends on everything being predictable.

When you start to loosen your grip, it feels unnatural at first. You may feel restless or uneasy, as though you are waiting for something to go wrong. That is the body's memory of uncertainty, not proof that you are unsafe. The goal is not to let go of control all at once. It is to begin noticing where it's costing you more than it's protecting you.

You can start small. Leave the dishes in the sink overnight. Let someone else take the lead on a project, even if they do it differently. Allow yourself to sit in silence without filling it with plans or tasks. These moments teach your nervous system that the world does not collapse when you stop managing it. They show you that peace can exist without control.

Over time, you begin to see that life doesn't need to be perfectly arranged for you to be okay. There is freedom in that realization. You can breathe easier when you no longer feel responsible for every outcome. You can connect more deeply when you stop trying to predict every emotion. You can feel joy again when you stop demanding certainty before you allow it.

Control will always whisper that it keeps you safe, but what it really keeps you is alone. Safety built on control is temporary. Real safety comes from trust. Trust that you can handle whatever happens. Trust that other people can meet you halfway. Trust that peace doesn't require perfection.

You don't have to abandon responsibility or structure to heal. You just have to stop worshipping them as your only source of security. The more you learn to live without micromanaging every moment, the more room there is for connection, rest, and ease.

The cost of control is your peace. The reward of letting go, even a little, is freedom.

FOUR

---

# *The Weight You Can't See*

Most people think exhaustion comes from doing too much, but often it comes from what we've been holding for too long. Not the tasks, the deadlines, or the daily noise of life, but the quiet weight that settles in your body after years of carrying emotions you never gave yourself permission to feel.

You carry it in ways that are easy to miss. The tightness in your shoulders that never fully relaxes. The shallow breath you take when you're thinking too far ahead. The tension that sits in your jaw when you're trying not to say what you really think. The ache in your stomach when something feels wrong but you pretend it's fine. None of these things seem significant on their own, but together they form a language your body has been speaking for years. It has been saying, "This is too much."

You've probably gotten used to it. Most people do. They tell themselves this is what adulthood feels like, that stress and fatigue are normal. You push through the heaviness, drink another cup of coffee, and keep moving. But deep down, you know something else is going on. The tiredness you feel isn't just physical. It's emotional. It's the wear and tear of pretending you're fine when you're not.

Your body keeps track of what your mind tries to ignore. Every time you swallow frustration instead of expressing it, your muscles tighten a little more. Every time you force a smile while your heart is aching, your breath becomes a little shallower. Every time you tell yourself to move on before you've had a chance to grieve, that grief settles somewhere inside you. It doesn't disappear; it waits.

We live in a culture that praises pushing through. The message is simple: work harder, stay strong, keep going. And for a while, you can. But the body has limits. It remembers what you try to forget. It keeps score of every emotion you avoided, every truth you swallowed, every moment you said yes when you wanted to say no. Over time, that record becomes weight. It's not visible, but it's heavy.

You might notice it as constant tension. You wake up tired no matter how much you sleep. You feel irritable for no reason. You can't focus, or you can't stop overthinking. You start to feel disconnected from the people around you, as though something inside you is always holding back. This is the body's way of saying, "I'm still carrying what you never let me release."

The weight you can't see often begins with good intentions. You tell yourself you don't have time to fall apart. You promise to deal with things later, when life calms down. But later never comes. Life keeps moving, and you keep carrying. You keep performing calm, pushing emotions aside, and convincing yourself that if you stay busy enough, you'll eventually feel better. But busyness doesn't heal what avoidance hides.

When you ignore your emotions, they don't go away. They shift form. They show up in your mood, your body, and your relationships. They make you tired in ways that sleep can't fix. They make you distant in ways you can't explain. They make your world feel heavy even when nothing is technically wrong.

You may not realize it, but your body has been trying to get your attention. That pressure in your chest when you think about certain people. The headache that appears every time you hold back tears. The fatigue that follows a conversation where you couldn't say what you wanted to say. These are signals, not random inconveniences. Your body isn't betraying you; it's communicating with you.

Healing begins when you start listening. You don't have to analyze every sensation or emotion, but you can start by noticing them. When your shoulders tense, pause. When you catch yourself holding your breath, exhale. When you feel tired for no reason, ask yourself what emotion might be hiding beneath the fatigue. The simple act of noticing begins to release what has been stored.

Sometimes the heaviness lifts in small ways. A deep breath that feels easier than usual. A walk that clears your mind. A cry that leaves you lighter. Other times, it takes longer. Emotions that have been buried for years take time to surface. You may not even know what all of them are yet, and that's okay. Your only job is to stop pretending they aren't there.

There is a difference between carrying responsibility and carrying emotion. Responsibility keeps life moving. Emotion keeps life meaningful. When you confuse the two, you spend all your energy holding things that don't belong to you. You become tired not from what you do, but from what you don't release.

Letting go of emotional weight is not about blaming anyone or reliving every painful moment. It's about acknowledging that you've been holding too much and deciding that you deserve to feel lighter. You begin to let go by choosing honesty over endurance, presence over pressure, and rest over relentless effort.

The weight you can't see will not disappear in one moment. It fades gradually, every time you tell the truth instead of saying you're fine, every time you breathe through tension instead of ignoring it, every time you give yourself permission to feel instead of pushing through. Slowly, the body learns that it no longer has to carry everything alone.

You may still have hard days. You may still get tired. But the difference is that now, tired will mean what it's supposed to mean — that you need rest, not that you are broken. As the weight lifts, even a little, you begin to remember what peace feels like. It's quieter than you expected. It's gentler. It's been waiting for you underneath all that effort, ready to rise the moment you stop mistaking control for strength and silence for peace.

You don't have to drop everything you're holding today. Just start by setting one thing down. One truth, one feeling, one expectation that isn't serving you anymore. Notice how your body responds. Notice the breath that follows. That's how you know you're beginning to heal.

FIVE

---

# *Emotional Ghosting*

There is a kind of disappearance that doesn't happen all at once. It happens slowly, quietly, through small choices made over time. You stop speaking up when something bothers you. You stop asking for help when you need it. You stop showing the full range of who you are. You start to fade out of your own life until one day you realize you have become a background character in your own story.

That is what emotional ghosting looks like. It is when you learn to retreat from your emotions before anyone else has the chance to reject them. You pull back from connection to stay safe. You minimize what you feel so you don't make others uncomfortable. You convince yourself that silence keeps the peace. And after enough time, you start believing that detachment is maturity.

Most people don't decide to ghost themselves on purpose. It begins as protection. Somewhere along the way, you learned that showing emotion made things harder. Maybe you were told you were too sensitive, too reactive, too dramatic. Maybe you tried to express a feeling and were met with anger, confusion, or dismissal. The lesson you learned was simple: it's easier to disconnect than to be misunderstood.

So you learned to shut things down before they start. You brush off hurt feelings before they grow. You swallow the lump in your throat before it turns into tears. You tell yourself you are being strong. And you are, but it's a kind of strength that costs you your aliveness.

At first, emotional ghosting feels peaceful. You tell yourself you've finally mastered composure. You don't get rattled, you don't overreact, you don't lose control. But peace that depends on avoidance isn't real peace. It's pause. It's holding your breath and calling it calm. It's convincing yourself that emptiness is serenity because at least it doesn't hurt.

The problem with avoiding your emotions is that they don't actually go anywhere. They simply lose their shape. Instead of showing up as sadness or anger, they come out as fatigue, frustration, and disconnection. You feel restless and detached, but you can't explain why. You go through life like you are behind glass, watching yourself from a distance. You can see what's happening, but you can't feel it.

Eventually, you start to miss yourself. You notice that your laughter sounds rehearsed. Your happiness feels polite. Your relationships feel safe but shallow. You realize you've built a life that looks fine on the outside but feels hollow on the inside. That hollow feeling is the cost of self-abandonment. You can only suppress emotion for so long before the distance becomes unbearable.

Reconnecting begins when you stop running from what you feel. It doesn't mean you have to unpack everything all at once. It simply means you stop editing yourself out of your own experiences. When something hurts, you let yourself admit it. When you feel angry, you let yourself explore why. When you are tired, you allow rest instead of forcing performance. Every time you honor a small truth, you take one step closer to yourself.

For a long time, emotional ghosting probably felt necessary. You had to keep things moving, stay composed, and be reliable. It served a purpose. It helped you survive. That version of you deserves gratitude, not shame. They were doing the best they could with what they had. But you don't have to keep living that way. You can be both responsible and real. You can be composed and connected. You can be peaceful and still present.

The truth is, emotional presence is not about feeling everything all the time. It's about not disappearing from yourself when you do. It's choosing to stay, even when staying feels uncomfortable. It's choosing honesty over performance, awareness over control, and curiosity over judgment.

The first time you practice staying, it might feel awkward. You may notice an urge to change the subject, make a joke, or distract yourself. That's okay. Old habits don't disappear quickly. Every time you notice yourself about to retreat and choose to stay instead, you are rewriting your story. You are telling your body and your mind that you no longer need to run.

Emotional ghosting ends when you start showing up for yourself the way you've always shown up for everyone else. When you stop waiting for permission to be human. When you start letting yourself feel joy without guilt and sadness without shame.

You were never meant to live halfway present. You were meant to feel deeply and still stay grounded, to express truth and still stay kind, to face pain and still stay hopeful.

You can come back to yourself slowly. With honesty. With patience. With compassion. Each time you choose to stay instead of disappear, you reclaim a piece of yourself that has been waiting to be found.

Because the opposite of disappearing is belonging.

Not to someone else, but to yourself. And that is where healing begins.

SIX

---

# Growing Up in Emotional Poverty

Some homes are full of noise but empty of connection. Others are quiet in a way that feels heavy. You can hear the tension in the air even when no one's speaking. You learn to listen for the sound of doors closing, the tone of footsteps, the shift in someone's breathing. You grow up reading the room instead of reading yourself.

That's what emotional poverty looks like. It's not always abuse or neglect. It's absence. The space between what you needed and what was given. It's growing up with food on the table and clothes on your back, yet still feeling hungry for something you couldn't name.

Emotional poverty teaches you to survive by guessing. You guess how to feel. You guess how to respond. You guess what love is supposed to look like. When no one models emotional honesty, you learn to improvise. You learn to suppress what doesn't fit. You learn that your feelings are inconveniences, not information.

Children in emotionally poor homes adapt fast. You become the observer, the peacekeeper, the invisible one. You get good at being fine. You learn that safety depends on being predictable, agreeable, or quiet. You stop asking for help because you learned that asking doesn't change much anyway.

Over time, that silence becomes your language. You don't talk about emotions because you were never shown how. The adults in your life may have been doing their best, but they were often just trying to hold it together themselves. They didn't have emotional fluency to teach you, so they handed you emotional fragments instead: phrases like "Stop crying," "You're fine," or "Be grateful." You internalized those as rules.

The result is a kind of emotional homelessness. You grow up but never quite feel at home inside yourself. You're always scanning for how you're supposed to feel, comparing your insides to other people's outsides, wondering why everyone else seems to have a manual for being human that you somehow missed.

As an adult, emotional poverty can look like achievement without fulfillment. You chase success because accomplishment feels safer than intimacy. You handle crises with ease but fall apart over stillness. You can care for others easily but struggle to let them care for you. You stay busy, productive, and outwardly stable, but underneath, you're still that kid waiting for someone to notice what you need.

This kind of upbringing doesn't ruin you, but it does shape you. It makes you independent long before you should have been. It makes you strong in ways that were never meant to be necessary. And it teaches you that needing something — comfort, affection, reassurance — is weakness. So you grow into an adult who knows how to provide everything except permission to feel.

The first step toward healing emotional poverty is recognition. To stop pretending it was normal. To name the gap for what it was not to blame, but to see. Emotional poverty doesn't mean your parents didn't love you. It means they didn't know how to love *through* emotion. They couldn't give what they never received. And in their effort to protect you from pain, they accidentally taught you to avoid connection.

Healing begins when you stop confusing emotional distance for stability. When you realize that feeling nothing isn't peace, it's deprivation. When you recognize that the absence of chaos isn't the same as the presence of safety.

You can learn what wasn't modeled. You can learn to speak emotions fluently, even if you grew up surrounded by silence. You can learn to comfort yourself instead of criticize yourself. You can learn to meet needs you were once taught to hide.

Emotional poverty isn't permanent. It's a condition of inheritance, not identity. It means you grew up in a place where love was real but limited, present but unspoken. It means you learned to survive without nourishment, but now you get to learn to thrive with it.

The wealth you were missing was never money, attention, or approval. It was emotional safety. And that's something you can now create. Mot by revisiting the past, but by choosing to feel in the present.

Because once you recognize what was missing, you can finally stop waiting for someone else to feed what's already growing inside you.

SEVEN

---

# *Love Me, Don't Leave Me*

There is a certain kind of fear that hides underneath even the strongest people. It isn't loud or dramatic. It doesn't always look like fear. It looks like trying too hard. It looks like apologizing too quickly. It looks like earning affection instead of receiving it. It's the quiet panic that says, "Please don't leave me."

Most people who carry this fear don't realize it's there. They think they're just being kind, thoughtful, or easygoing. They pride themselves on being dependable. But under the surface, there's an anxiety that never fully turns off. It whispers that love can be lost at any moment, that closeness is temporary, that being yourself might be too much.

This fear doesn't appear out of nowhere. It begins in the early spaces where love and acceptance were first learned. Maybe you grew up with love that had conditions. Maybe approval came when you achieved something, behaved a certain way, or made life easier for everyone else. Maybe you were taught that love could be withdrawn if you disappointed someone. When that kind of pattern is repeated often enough, it becomes an emotional rule: connection is not guaranteed.

So you learn to manage it. You become hyperaware of other people's moods. You learn to read faces and tones before words are even spoken. You learn to avoid conflict, not because you are afraid of disagreement, but because you are afraid of disconnection. You carry the weight of keeping relationships stable, even when the other person isn't doing their part. You tell yourself that love takes work, but what you're really doing is carrying the relationship by yourself.

That is what this fear does. It turns love into labor. You start working to be easy to love. You hide the parts of yourself that might cause tension. You say yes when you want to say no. You shrink your emotions so no one feels uncomfortable around you. You apologize for things that aren't your fault. You treat love like a job you might get fired from.

It's exhausting, but it feels safer than being left.

This kind of emotional pattern can show up anywhere. In romantic relationships, friendships, families, or work environments. It shows up every time you overextend yourself to be accepted. It shows up every time you feel anxious after a disagreement and rush to fix it, even if you weren't wrong. It shows up every time you replay a conversation in your mind, wondering if you said too much. It shows up every time someone pulls away and your first instinct is to chase, not because you want control, but because you're terrified of abandonment.

What's painful about this pattern is that it's self-reinforcing. The more you try to hold on, the more anxious you become. The more anxious you become, the harder you work to prove your worth. The harder you work, the more invisible your needs become. Eventually, you realize that you're loved for how dependable you are, but not for how you actually feel.

It's easy to mislabel this pattern as people-pleasing, but it's deeper than that. It's attachment built on survival. When love has ever felt uncertain, your nervous system treats closeness as both comfort and risk. You want it, but you also brace for it to end. So even in good relationships, you never feel fully safe.

The healing process starts with awareness. You begin to notice when you're trying to earn affection. You begin to notice when you're taking responsibility for someone else's emotions. You begin to notice the quiet panic that rises when someone pulls away. Instead of acting on that panic, you pause. You remind yourself that love doesn't have to be earned, and that space doesn't always mean rejection.

That pause is powerful. It interrupts the old rule that says you have to chase love to keep it. It gives you time to choose a different response. You can take a breath, sit with the discomfort, and remind yourself that your worth isn't dependent on someone else's approval. It won't feel natural at first. You will feel restless and uncertain. But the more you practice, the more your body learns that not everyone leaves.

The truth is, people who love you don't need you to be perfect. They don't need you to always agree or always fix things. They just need you to be real. And the people who disappear when you stop performing were never staying for the right reasons. It's painful, but it's also clarifying. Every relationship you lose to honesty makes space for one that's built on truth.

Over time, you begin to understand that love is not something you earn. It's something you experience when you allow yourself to be known. You can still be kind and giving without being self-erasing. You can still care deeply without carrying everything alone. You can still want connection without losing yourself inside it.

The fear of being left doesn't vanish overnight. It may still whisper in moments of silence or tension. But the more you honor yourself, the quieter it becomes. You start to realize that the love you've been chasing has been trying to reach you all along. It's the love that comes from within. The one that says, "Even if they go, I will stay."

That kind of love can't be taken away, because it doesn't depend on anyone else. It's the love that grows when you finally stop negotiating your worth and start believing that you were never too much to be loved in the first place.

EIGHT

---

# *The Good Child Syndrome*

When you grow up in emotional poverty, you learn early that comfort doesn't come freely. You figure out that being easy to love is the safest way to survive. You become the good one. The calm one. The helper. The peacemaker. The child who never makes things harder than they already are.

At first, it seems like a choice, but it isn't. It's instinct. You read the room and adapt to keep things steady. If the adults are stressed, you stay quiet. If they're sad, you make them smile. If they're angry, you disappear. You learn that love feels safest when it isn't disrupted, and that keeping everyone else okay is how you stay safe too.

The good child becomes fluent in self-erasure. You don't ask for much. You learn to solve your own problems. You take pride in being low maintenance. You measure your worth in how little space you take up. And everyone praises you for it.

"You're such a good kid." "You're so mature for your age." "You're such a big help."

No one realizes that what they're praising is your coping mechanism.

Good children grow up fast. You learn to anticipate what people need before they say it. You sense the mood in a room like a weather report. You take responsibility for things that were never yours. And every time someone calls you reliable, a part of you feels both proud and unseen.

As you get older, the pattern doesn't disappear. It just changes form. You become the person everyone depends on. You fix things before they break. You listen to everyone else's problems but hide your own. You hold your emotions like secrets, convinced that sharing them would make you a burden. You carry the weight of other people's comfort like it's your purpose.

What people see as strength is often fear in disguise. You're not calm because you're peaceful. You're calm because you're practiced. You're not patient because you don't feel anger. You're patient because anger once felt dangerous. You're not easygoing because you're carefree. You're easygoing because conflict still feels like threat.

The problem with being the good child is that it works. You get love, but it's conditional. You get approval, but it costs authenticity. You feel valued, but not known. And over time, that quiet ache of invisibility starts to grow. You start to realize that the role you built to stay safe has also kept you small.

As an adult, this pattern shows up as over-functioning. You take care of everyone and everything. You have trouble resting because rest feels selfish. You have trouble saying no because you don't want to disappoint anyone. You think constantly about how others will feel, and almost never about what you need.

You might even call it being "responsible," but responsibility isn't the same as self-abandonment. You don't owe the world constant calm. You don't have to earn your right to exist by being agreeable.

Healing from the good child pattern begins with permission. Permission to need things. Permission to disappoint people. Permission to stop fixing what isn't yours. The moment you stop earning love through effort is the moment you begin to feel it for real.

You don't have to stop being kind. You just have to stop confusing kindness with compliance. You don't have to stop being dependable. You just have to stop carrying what isn't yours to hold. You don't have to stop being good. You just have to start being whole.

There's a difference between goodness that comes from fear and goodness that comes from truth. Fear says, "If I stop pleasing, I'll be rejected." Truth says, "If I stay authentic, the right people will stay." One drains you. The other restores you.

Being the good child was never a flaw. It was an adaptation. It was how you created stability in an unstable world. You did what you had to do to stay safe. But now, safety looks different. It's not silence or control. It's honesty. It's rest. It's balance.

You don't have to unlearn your goodness. You just have to let it include yourself.

When you finally do, life starts to feel lighter. Relationships become mutual instead of one-sided. Rest stops feeling wrong. Love stops feeling like work. And you stop feeling like you have to earn what was always meant to be given freely.

NINE

---

# Inherited Armor

Not every wound starts with you. Some are passed down quietly, tucked into the way your family handled emotion, conflict, and love. You inherit your eye color, your voice, and sometimes, your fear.

Families pass down more than stories. They pass down survival strategies. You learn what love looks like by watching how people express it or avoid it. You learn what strength means by watching who is allowed to cry. You learn what safety feels like by noticing what happens when someone gets angry. These lessons don't come from lectures. They come from patterns repeated so often they start to feel like truth.

In many families, emotions were seen as weaknesses that could open the door to chaos. So they built armor instead. Some built it from silence. Others from control. Others from humor or work or perfection. That armor kept life predictable, but it also made closeness difficult. When you grow up inside that kind of pattern, distance starts to feel like peace.

Your parents or grandparents might not have called it trauma. They would have called it survival. They didn't talk about feelings because talking never changed anything. They stayed busy because stillness felt dangerous. They held everything inside because they thought that was strength. What they didn't realize was that the armor they built to protect themselves would one day keep their children from feeling connected.

If you look closely, you can see how the armor took shape in your life. Maybe it's the way you freeze when someone raises their voice, or how you work yourself to exhaustion so you don't have to feel vulnerable. Maybe it's the way you avoid conflict by overexplaining, or how you only cry in private because you think no one can handle it. The patterns look different in every family, but the purpose is always the same. Protection.

It's easy to look back with resentment and think, "Why didn't they do better?" But most of the time, they couldn't. The people who taught you to suppress emotions were often carrying the same burden themselves. They didn't know how to process pain. They only knew how to prevent it. They didn't mean to pass down avoidance. They were doing their best to keep the family from breaking.

That doesn't make the effects any less real. The armor that once kept them safe now keeps you disconnected. It's what makes you feel like you have to be strong all the time. It's what makes you hesitate before being honest. It's what makes you proud of independence but secretly tired of isolation.

Recognizing that you inherited this doesn't mean you're doomed to keep it. It means you finally have the chance to end it. The cycle only continues when no one questions it. The moment you stop mistaking emotional distance for strength, you start to break the pattern.

Healing inherited armor requires compassion, not blame. You can't tear it off in anger. You have to loosen it with understanding. You can look at your parents and see that they were trying to love you in the only way they knew how. You can honor what they gave you — endurance, work ethic, loyalty — while releasing what they couldn't yet offer — vulnerability, softness, safety.

You might even find gratitude in the realization that they gave you the tools to survive, and you're now using those same tools to learn how to live. You can keep the discipline and drop the defensiveness. You can keep the resilience and release the rigidity. You can keep the lessons and change the language.

When you do, you begin to feel something your family may never have known. Peace without numbness.

You stop repeating the silence. You start speaking gently, even when it's hard. You stop pretending you're fine. You start letting yourself be real. And in doing that, you teach your children or the people around you something new: that strength and softness can live in the same place.

The armor you inherited doesn't need to be destroyed. It just needs to be outgrown. You can still carry the best of where you came from without carrying the weight of what they couldn't heal.

Because every generation hands down something. The question is whether it will be protection or presence.

When you choose to heal, you give the next generation the gift your family never had. The safety to feel.

TEN

---

# *The Illusion of Strength*

Strength is one of the most misunderstood qualities we aspire to. We talk about it like it's the highest compliment a person can receive. You're so strong. You're so resilient. You're so composed. What most people don't realize is that the version of strength they're praising often has nothing to do with peace. It's survival in disguise.

For many people, strength was the only acceptable way to exist. You were told to be tough, to push through, to keep going. Maybe no one ever said the words directly, but you saw how it worked. The people who stayed calm were respected. The ones who cried were ignored or criticized. The ones who struggled were told to pull themselves together. The lesson was clear: showing emotion meant weakness.

So you got strong. You stopped complaining. You stopped crying. You learned how to do things alone. You learned how to push through pain quietly and call it growth. On the outside, it looked impressive. You became capable, reliable, unshakable. On the inside, it felt lonely.

The illusion of strength is that it keeps you safe. It makes you believe that independence is power and that needing others is dangerous. It convinces you that being vulnerable will undo you, that being soft will make people take advantage of you, that being open will make you lose control. So you hold yourself together so tightly that you stop letting anyone in.

But true strength has nothing to do with how well you can hide your emotions. It's measured by how willing you are to face them. The strongest people are not the ones who never fall apart. They are the ones who stop pretending they don't need to.

There's a kind of courage that doesn't look like grit or endurance. It's quieter. It's the courage to tell the truth. The courage to cry without apology. The courage to admit that you are tired of being fine all the time. That kind of strength doesn't shout. It softens. It breathes. It allows space for humanity.

When you've spent years equating strength with composure, it's hard to unlearn. You may feel uncomfortable when others see you upset. You may feel shame when you ask for help. You may feel weak when you take a break. That discomfort isn't proof that you're doing something wrong. It's a sign that you're doing something different.

You might even notice how deeply this illusion has shaped your relationships. People see your confidence and assume you don't need support. They admire your independence but rarely check if you're okay. They depend on your steadiness but don't realize it costs you your peace. Meanwhile, you stay quiet because asking for help feels like burdening someone. You keep performing strength while quietly hoping someone will notice that you're tired.

That's the trap of the illusion. The more you appear strong, the less people offer you care. And the less care you receive, the more you double down on being strong. It becomes a cycle of invisibility, where your resilience isolates you from the intimacy you secretly crave.

Breaking that cycle doesn't mean becoming fragile. It means becoming honest. It means letting people see your humanity instead of just your composure. It means redefining strength so it includes softness, compassion, and rest.

There is a difference between strength that protects and strength that imprisons. Protective strength says, "I can handle this." Imprisoning strength says, "I have to handle this." One comes from choice. The other comes from fear. The moment you begin choosing when to be strong and when to be open, you start reclaiming balance.

Letting yourself rest is not weakness. Letting yourself cry is not regression. Letting yourself receive help is not dependence. These are the practices that make strength sustainable. You were never meant to hold everything alone.

Even the strongest structures crumble under the weight of constant pressure.

It can feel strange to start living this way, especially if you were raised to believe that control equals safety. But real strength doesn't come from control. It comes from trust — the trust that you can survive emotions instead of avoiding them, that you can depend on others without losing yourself, that you can still stand tall without needing to be invincible.

When you finally stop performing strength, you start to experience peace. You discover that being strong isn't about what you can endure. It's about what you're willing to release. It's about knowing when to hold on and when to let go. It's about choosing honesty over appearances, connection over perfection, truth over image.

There is a calm that only comes after you stop pretending to be unbreakable. It doesn't come from control or composure. It comes from authenticity. From being able to look at yourself and say, "I'm strong enough to feel."

That's real strength — not the kind that hardens you, but the kind that lets you stay open. Not the kind that hides pain, but the kind that faces it. Not the kind that earns admiration, but the kind that builds peace.

And once you know that kind of strength, you never go back to the illusion again.

ELEVEN

---

# The Myth of Overreacting

If you've ever been told you were "too sensitive," you know how quickly those words can shape you. At first, they sting. Later, they settle in. You begin to question every emotion you have. You start editing your reactions before they reach your face. You become skilled at noticing what you feel, but even better at hiding it. You convince yourself that control is maturity, that calmness is power, and that the best way to stay safe is to feel less.

This is how emotional suppression begins for so many people. Not through malice, but through misunderstanding. You were never trying to be dramatic. You were trying to be honest about what hurt. You were trying to show that something mattered. But somewhere along the way, someone told you that your truth was inconvenient. They might not have meant to wound you. Maybe they were overwhelmed, distracted, or uncomfortable with emotion. But their reaction taught you a message that stuck: feeling deeply is a problem.

Over time, you learn to anticipate that dismissal before it even happens. You feel something rising and tell yourself to calm down. You rehearse conversations in your head to make sure you sound reasonable. You catch yourself apologizing for your tone, your tears, or even your silence. You call it being considerate, but really it's self-protection. You are trying to make your emotions smaller so they fit into spaces that never made room for them.

The problem is that emotions do not disappear when you minimize them. They simply lose their shape. The sadness you ignore becomes exhaustion. The anger you swallow turns into resentment. The anxiety you deny turns into control. The joy you hold back turns into distance. The very feelings you tried to manage end up managing you.

When you grow up being told you overreact, you start to distrust your own perceptions. You gaslight yourself before anyone else can. You tell yourself you're fine when you're not. You downplay your pain so others won't think you're dramatic. You second-guess your instincts even when something feels off. That internal conflict creates a quiet kind of suffering — the kind where you are present but disconnected, speaking but never fully saying what you mean.

The truth is that there is no such thing as an overreaction when it comes to emotion. There are only responses that make sense in context. When a situation touches an old wound, the feeling it stirs will always be bigger than the moment itself. That doesn't make you unstable. It makes you human. It means your system remembers. It means there's something inside you asking to be seen.

Emotions are not right or wrong. They are information. They tell you what feels safe and what doesn't, what feels aligned and what doesn't. When you start labeling certain emotions as overreactions, you shut down your own internal guidance system. You teach yourself to ignore the very signals designed to help you navigate life.

This is why so many people struggle with boundaries. They don't know when something has crossed a line until long after it happens, because they've trained themselves not to feel the discomfort in real time. They notice the tension later — in their headaches, their irritability, their fatigue — but not in the moment, because they've spent years silencing their body's early warnings.

Healing from this begins with validation. You have to start telling yourself the truth that no one else told you. You have to remind yourself that your emotions make sense, even when they feel inconvenient. You can acknowledge that your feelings are real without acting on every impulse they bring. Feeling something strongly doesn't mean you are irrational. It means you care. It means you are alive.

The goal isn't to justify every emotion or indulge every mood. It's to stop shaming yourself for having them. You can learn to pause without suppressing. You can learn to breathe before responding. You can learn to question your reactions with curiosity instead of criticism. The more you do this, the more your emotions begin to trust you again. They soften. They stop shouting because they know you're listening.

This takes time. At first, allowing yourself to feel can make you anxious. You might worry about being too much. You might fear judgment from others. But eventually, you start to notice that people who truly care about you don't need you to dilute yourself to stay close. They want your honesty more than your performance. They feel safer around you when you stop managing every expression.

And just as importantly, you start to feel safer within yourself. You no longer interpret emotion as danger. You start to see it as data — information that helps you make choices that align with peace rather than performance.

The next time someone implies that you are overreacting, you can pause before shrinking. You can remember that it's not always about being too much. Sometimes it's about being in the presence of someone who feels too little.

Your sensitivity isn't a flaw to correct. It's a compass. It's the part of you that notices the world more deeply, that feels truth before logic can explain it. The world needs that kind of sensitivity. You need it too.

When you stop judging your emotions and start listening to them, you begin to rebuild the trust you lost with yourself. That's when strength starts to feel different. It's no longer the quiet endurance of holding everything in. It's the steady confidence of knowing you can feel anything and still stay whole.

TWELVE

---

# *Survival Mode*

There is a certain rhythm that takes over when life feels unpredictable. You stop thinking about what you need and start focusing on what needs to be done. You wake up and immediately start scanning for problems, managing other people's moods, or preparing for what could go wrong. You move through the day like a soldier on watch - alert, efficient, capable. On the surface, it looks like discipline. Beneath it, it's survival.

Most people in survival mode don't realize they're living that way. It feels normal. It feels like being responsible, like being driven, like being strong. But if you pay attention, there's a difference between being productive and being on guard. Productivity comes from purpose. Survival comes from fear. And fear is exhausting.

Survival mode isn't just mental; it's physical. It lives in the body. It's the tight shoulders, the clenched jaw, the restless sleep. It's the shallow breath you take without realizing it. It's the sense that you're always running a few seconds ahead of the present moment. Your nervous system has learned that safety depends on staying ready.

That readiness might have helped you once. Maybe you grew up in an environment where calm could turn into chaos in an instant, so you learned to stay alert. Maybe you've experienced loss or betrayal and now your body is always waiting for the next impact. Maybe you've just spent so many years in high-stress environments that your system doesn't remember what peace feels like. Whatever the reason, your body learned a simple rule: never fully relax.

The problem is that the body can't tell the difference between a real threat and an emotional one. It reacts to both the same way — by tightening, bracing, preparing to fight, flee, or shut down. Over time, this becomes a habit. Even when things are fine, you feel restless. Even when life is stable, you find something to fix. Stillness makes you anxious because stillness feels unsafe.

Survival mode keeps you busy. It makes you believe that movement equals safety, that control equals peace. You fill your calendar, your mind, and your home with things to do. You plan for every possibility. You double-check every detail. But beneath all that effort is one unspoken fear: if I stop paying attention, something bad will happen.

That belief runs deep. It shows up in subtle ways. You might have trouble resting because rest feels unearned. You might find it hard to celebrate achievements because you're already focused on the next challenge. You might struggle to let others help you because dependence feels like danger. You might even feel uncomfortable in moments of calm, as though you've forgotten how to just exist.

Survival mode steals presence. It keeps you locked in anticipation. You can't enjoy the moment you're in because your mind is always one step ahead, bracing for impact. You spend your life trying to prevent pain instead of experiencing peace.

And the hardest part is that it works — for a while. You stay functional. You get things done. You handle crises better than most. People praise your reliability. They admire your composure. They have no idea that underneath all that control is a body that hasn't felt truly relaxed in years.

The longer you live this way, the more disconnected you become from what you feel. Your emotions get pushed to the side because feeling them might slow you down. You tell yourself you'll deal with them later, but later never comes. Eventually, you stop realizing how much you've adapted. You call it personality. You say, "I just don't get stressed easily," even as your body shows signs of chronic tension. You call it high standards. You call it focus. But it's vigilance.

The first step out of survival mode is recognition. You can't change what you don't see. Begin by noticing the small moments when your body reacts even though there's no real threat. Notice how your chest tightens when someone disagrees with you. Notice how your mind races when things are quiet. Notice how you fill silence with tasks or noise. These are clues that your body still believes it's responsible for preventing chaos.

When you start noticing these moments, the goal isn't to judge them. It's to understand them. Your body isn't malfunctioning; it's protecting you. It's been doing exactly what it learned to do. The problem is that it never got the message that you're safe now. Healing begins when you start sending that message.

You can start with the smallest acts of permission. Take a breath and let your shoulders drop, even for a moment. Sit still without checking your phone. Let a task remain unfinished and remind yourself that the world won't collapse because of it. These aren't just relaxation techniques; they're signals to your nervous system that you are no longer in danger.

The truth is, survival mode was never meant to be a lifestyle. It was meant to be a short-term response to a threat. When it becomes the default, it starts to take things from you. Your rest, your creativity, your emotional depth, your capacity for joy. The longer you live in that state, the more life starts to feel like endurance instead of experience.

But the body can relearn safety. It takes time, patience, and practice, but it's possible. Each moment you slow down, each time you breathe deeply, each instance where you allow rest without guilt, you are retraining your system to believe that calm is not danger. You are showing yourself that peace is not the same as vulnerability.

Eventually, your body starts to trust you again. The constant edge softens. The tension eases. The world starts to feel less like a threat and more like a place you belong.

You don't have to abandon everything that made you capable. You just have to stop confusing vigilance with virtue. You don't have to lose your drive or your focus. You just have to remember that life isn't something to survive. It's something to feel.

And the moment you start believing that, survival mode begins to loosen its grip. What replaces it isn't weakness. It's freedom — the kind that comes when you finally stop running from what you feel and start trusting that you can handle whatever comes next.

THIRTEEN

---

# *The Walls We Build*

Every person builds walls at some point. Some are built out of necessity, others out of fear, and most without even realizing it. They start as protection — small, simple acts of self-preservation meant to keep you safe from pain, rejection, or chaos. But over time, those protective layers grow thicker. The walls that once made you feel secure begin to separate you from the very things you need most: love, peace, and connection.

No one sets out to live behind walls. They form quietly. They form when you learn that speaking up makes people angry. They form when you cry and someone tells you to stop. They form when you share your feelings and are met with silence instead of support. They form when disappointment starts to feel predictable. You build walls to avoid getting hurt again, and before long, safety becomes another word for distance.

Sometimes the wall looks like control. You plan, organize, and overthink because certainty feels safer than trust. Sometimes it looks like silence. You stay quiet because vulnerability feels risky. Sometimes it looks like perfection. You try to get everything right so no one will have a reason to reject you. And sometimes it looks like indifference, the mask you wear when you want to care but can't handle the risk of caring fully.

The wall always has a purpose. It was built to protect something soft. Maybe it's your hope. Maybe it's your heart. Maybe it's the part of you that once believed love was supposed to feel safe. Whatever it is, the wall kept it hidden so you could keep moving. For a long time, it worked. You avoided conflict. You avoided rejection. You avoided pain. What you didn't realize was that you were also avoiding joy.

Walls don't discriminate. They block out everything. The bad and the good, the hurt and the healing. They keep you safe, but they also keep you numb. They give you control, but they take away connection. They protect your heart, but they also prevent it from expanding. The longer you live behind them, the heavier life starts to feel.

At first, you might tell yourself that you prefer it this way. You say you like your space, your independence, your quiet. And some of that is true. But deep down, there's a part of you that misses being seen. There's a part that longs for real closeness, the kind where you can stop pretending and simply exist. That longing isn't weakness. It's proof that you're still alive underneath the armor.

The hardest thing about taking down your walls is that they worked. They kept you from falling apart. They gave you control when the world felt unpredictable. They allowed you to survive situations that could have broken you. For that, they deserve gratitude. But what kept you safe is now keeping you stuck. You can't heal what you keep hidden. You can't connect through walls built to keep others out.

Letting the walls down doesn't mean exposing everything or trusting everyone. It means allowing light and air to reach the places that have been closed off for too long. It means softening your edges just enough to let truth in. It means learning how to feel again without letting fear dictate the terms.

The process is slow. It starts with small moments of honesty, admitting to yourself when you are hurt instead of brushing it off, sharing a piece of truth with someone safe, or allowing yourself to cry without apologizing. Every time you do, you create a crack in the wall. Those cracks are not failures. They are signs of healing. They let you breathe again.

You might feel exposed at first. You might even want to retreat. That's natural. Vulnerability feels foreign when you've lived in defense for years. But each time you resist the urge to hide, you remind yourself that not all openness leads to pain. Some of it leads to connection. Some of it leads to peace. Some of it leads to the life you've been missing.

As the walls come down, you begin to see that safety doesn't come from hiding. It comes from trust. Trust in your ability to handle emotion, trust in your strength to survive pain, and trust in the people who prove themselves worthy of your openness. Real safety isn't about avoiding hurt. It's about knowing that if hurt comes, you will still be okay.

That is the shift this book has been leading you toward. You have spent years protecting yourself from emotion because no one taught you how to feel it without falling apart. Now, you're beginning to see that feeling doesn't destroy you. Avoiding it does. The walls may have helped you survive, but they were never meant to be permanent.

You can thank them for what they gave you. Then you can begin to step beyond them — slowly, gently, and on your own terms. Because the moment you stop living behind what protected you, you finally step into what can heal you.

FOURTEEN

---

# *What Your Feelings Are Trying to Tell You*

For most of your life, emotions probably felt like interruptions. They arrived at the worst times and stayed longer than you wanted them to. They distracted you when you were trying to focus and made you uncomfortable when you wanted to stay composed. No one ever taught you that they were messengers. You were taught to manage them, hide them, or rise above them. So you did. You kept moving, thinking that maturity meant staying unaffected.

But emotions are not interruptions. They are communication. They are how your mind and body speak to each other. Every feeling carries a message. It tells you something about what is happening inside you and around you. Emotions are not there to control you; they are there to guide you. The problem is that when you've spent years trying not to feel, you forget how to listen.

Most people were never taught how to interpret what they feel. They were told that anger is bad, sadness is weakness, fear is irrational, and joy is something you have to earn. When you grow up with that kind of conditioning, you learn to separate from your emotional life. You don't stop having feelings; you just stop trusting them. You label some as good and others as bad. You praise yourself for staying calm, even when calm really means numb. You become fluent in analysis but illiterate in emotion.

The truth is that emotions are neither good nor bad. They are data. They show you what matters. They alert you when something isn't right. They reveal what needs attention. When you understand them, they stop feeling like chaos and start feeling like clarity.

Anger, for example, often points to boundaries that have been crossed. It's not just rage or irritation; it's a signal that something feels unfair or out of alignment. When you ignore anger, it doesn't disappear. It turns inward, showing up as resentment, fatigue, or bitterness. When you listen to it, you begin to see where you've been tolerating what doesn't serve you.

Sadness shows you what you value. It reminds you of what mattered enough to lose. It slows you down long enough to process change. When you dismiss sadness, you lose the opportunity to grieve, and grief is what clears space for new life.

Fear tells you that something feels uncertain. It's not always a warning to stop. Sometimes it's an invitation to prepare. It's your body's way of saying, "Pay attention." When you run from fear, you also run from growth.

Even joy carries information. It shows you where you feel most alive, what you're meant to move toward, what restores your spirit. When you downplay joy because you're afraid it won't last, you cut yourself off from the energy that heals you.

The point isn't to obey your emotions blindly. It's to be curious about what they are trying to say. Every feeling is trying to tell you something. Anxiety might be asking for safety. Frustration might be asking for rest. Loneliness might be asking for connection. These messages are simple once you slow down enough to listen.

Listening takes practice. At first, it might feel like you're opening a box that's been sealed for years. Everything rushes out at once. Old pain, forgotten memories, unprocessed grief, it can feel like too much. But that's normal. You're not falling apart. You're finally feeling what you've been carrying.

You don't have to unpack every emotion at once. You don't even have to understand them right away. Start with noticing. When something rises in your chest, instead of pushing it away, name it. You can say, "That's anger," or "That's sadness," or "That's anxiety." Naming an emotion separates it from your identity. You're not an angry person; you're a person feeling anger. You're not an anxious person; you're a person experiencing anxiety. This small shift changes everything.

When you give emotions names, they begin to soften. They stop being abstract forces and start becoming familiar signals. Over time, you'll start to recognize patterns. You'll know what your body feels like when you're stressed, what your heart does when you're lonely, what your energy feels like when you're overwhelmed. Awareness becomes your anchor.

It's also important to remember that emotions aren't logical. They don't always match the size of the situation because they're not just responding to the present moment, they're responding to your history. When you find yourself reacting strongly, pause before you judge it. Ask yourself, "What might this remind me of?" Sometimes the emotion belongs to an old story that never got closure. Listening is how you begin to find that closure.

As you learn to interpret your emotions, you'll notice that they stop feeling like something to control and start feeling like something to trust. You'll realize that they're not trying to ruin your life; they're trying to restore balance. They're signals of what needs to heal, not proof that you're broken.

Your emotions are not a burden. They are a language. They have been waiting for you to remember how to speak them.

You don't need to fix every feeling you have. You just need to hear it. The act of listening itself is healing. Because when you listen, you stop abandoning yourself. And that is how emotional awareness becomes emotional safety.

The goal is not to feel good all the time. The goal is to feel truthfully. Because when you do, even the hard emotions become less frightening. You realize they're not here to control you. They're here to connect you back to life.

And that's the beginning of peace.

FIFTEEN

---

# *Naming What Hurts*

There is a moment in every healing journey when awareness turns into truth. It's the moment when you stop describing your pain as stress or exhaustion and start calling it what it really is. Hurt. Grief. Disappointment. Loneliness. Fear. The names we give our pain are what begin to set it free.

For years, you might have talked around your emotions. You said you were tired when you were really heartbroken. You said you were fine when you were really angry. You said you were busy when you were really overwhelmed. You learned to speak in coded language because that felt safer than being honest. But coded language can't heal what it hides.

Naming what hurts doesn't mean dramatizing it. It means telling the truth about what's been sitting quietly inside you. It's the difference between saying, "I'm okay," and saying, "I feel ignored," or "I feel scared," or "I feel unseen." Honesty isn't weakness. It's direction. It's what turns confusion into clarity.

Many people avoid naming their pain because they're afraid it will make it more real. They think that if they put words to it, it will grow bigger. But the opposite is true. What you name, you contain. What you refuse to name, contains you.

You can't heal something that stays undefined. The emotions you never identify become the weight you can't explain. You feel drained but don't know why. You feel off but can't point to what's wrong. That's what happens when hurt has no name. It becomes background noise. Always present, never addressed.

Sometimes we avoid naming pain because it feels disloyal. You might think, "My parents did their best," or "My partner means well," or "It's not that bad." But naming your hurt isn't about blaming anyone. It's about acknowledging your reality. You can hold compassion for others and still tell the truth about how their actions affected you. Denial doesn't protect anyone; it just delays healing.

Other times, you avoid naming pain because you've convinced yourself it's selfish. You tell yourself other people have it worse, so you minimize what you feel. You say things like, "I shouldn't be upset about this," or "I should be over it by now." But pain doesn't respond to comparison. It only responds to compassion. You don't need permission to acknowledge what hurts. You just need honesty.

The act of naming pain is an act of courage. It's saying, "This mattered. This affected me. This shaped me." When you name your hurt, you're not creating new wounds, you're cleaning the ones that already exist. You're letting air and light reach the places that have been shut off.

It might feel uncomfortable at first. Naming pain means revisiting things you've tried to forget. But honesty is never the enemy. It's the first sign that you're strong enough to stop pretending. It's the moment you start to choose peace over performance.

You can start small. Take a quiet moment and ask yourself, "What am I really feeling?" Don't analyze it. Don't explain it away. Just listen. If you can't find the right word, describe the sensation. Maybe your chest feels heavy. Maybe your stomach is tight. Maybe your throat feels blocked. These physical clues often point to the emotion underneath. When you name it, even privately, you reclaim a piece of power that silence took from you.

Naming pain doesn't make you fragile. It makes you aware. It allows you to see what your body and heart have been carrying. It lets you set down the burdens that were never meant to be permanent.

Over time, as you practice naming what hurts, you start to notice patterns. You recognize familiar feelings before they grow overwhelming. You understand the difference between anger and sadness, between fear and guilt. You begin to speak your emotional truth fluently. And that fluency is what brings relief.

It's not about finding perfect words. It's about honest ones. Words like lonely, tired, disappointed, hopeful, or lost. Words that capture how your inner world feels, even if no one else understands. Once your pain has a name, it can be met. It can be soothed. It can begin to move.

You've spent years protecting yourself from your feelings because you thought they would drown you. The truth is that naming them is what helps you swim. It gives them edges. It gives you direction. It gives you understanding.

You can't heal what you keep vague. You can only heal what you're willing to name.

SIXTEEN

---

# *The Body Keeps the Story*

Every emotion you've ever had left a trace somewhere in your body. Some came and went easily. Others stayed. The ones you ignored, silenced, or denied didn't disappear. They settled into muscles, joints, and patterns of tension. They became the tightness in your chest, the knot in your stomach, the stiffness in your shoulders.

The body remembers what the mind forgets.

When something painful happens, your body reacts before you even have time to think. Your heart races, your breath shortens, your muscles brace. That reaction is natural. It's your body preparing to protect you. The problem comes when the body never gets the signal that the threat has passed. The event ends, but the tension remains. It becomes part of your baseline — invisible, constant, and exhausting.

Over time, those unprocessed emotions start to shape how you live. You hold your breath without realizing it. You sit with your jaw clenched. You stay busy to outrun the restlessness that settles in your body whenever you're still. You might even confuse that tension for personality. You say things like, "I just can't relax," or "I'm always on edge," as though it's who you are, not what you've been carrying.

When you've spent years trying not to feel, your body learns to tighten as a form of control. It tries to contain what was never allowed to move through. Every muscle that stays tense is a story unfinished, a sentence that never got to end.

But the body doesn't store pain to punish you. It does it to protect you. It keeps holding the emotion until it senses it's safe to release it. That's why certain moments — a song, a smell, a piece of silence — can suddenly bring tears you didn't expect. The body finally found a moment that felt safe enough to speak.

This is what healing really looks like. It's not just emotional insight. It's physical release. It's learning to notice what your body is trying to say when words fall short.

You might start by simply paying attention. When you feel anxious, ask yourself where you feel it. Maybe it's a flutter in your chest or a tightness in your throat. When you feel angry, notice your hands, your jaw, your breathing. When you feel sadness, notice the weight behind your eyes or the heaviness in your chest. Awareness is the first step.

Then comes permission. Let yourself breathe. Deeply. Not to control or fix anything, but to give your body proof that it can soften. Movement helps too. Stretching, walking, dancing, crying — these are ways your body speaks when language isn't enough. You don't have to intellectualize it. You just have to listen.

Healing through the body is not dramatic. It's often quiet and ordinary. It's taking a deep breath in the middle of a hard conversation. It's lying on the floor for five minutes and letting yourself feel heavy. It's noticing that you've been holding your breath and finally exhaling. It's letting your shoulders drop after years of holding them high. These small acts tell your body that it doesn't have to fight anymore.

Sometimes release feels emotional. Tears come without warning. Your voice shakes when you finally tell the truth. You feel anger or sadness move through you in waves. None of this means you're falling apart. It means the story that's been stuck inside you is finally being told.

It's important to move gently with yourself. The body doesn't respond well to force. You can't rush its healing. You can only meet it with patience. The same way you would listen to a friend who's been holding in pain for years, you listen to your body, without judgment, without interruption.

You don't need to remember every story your body carries. You just need to create space for it to speak. When you stop fighting your physical sensations, they start to shift on their own. What used to feel like anxiety might start to feel like energy. What used to feel like fatigue might start to feel like release.

The goal isn't to control your body, but to reconnect with it. To remember that it's not the enemy. It's the home that held you through every storm. It carried what your mind couldn't. It waited for you to return.

When you finally begin to listen, you'll notice that your body is always honest. It doesn't lie the way the mind can. It doesn't rationalize or overthink. It simply tells you the truth, through tension, through breath, through the way it softens when you allow presence.

Healing is not only in the words you speak. It's in the breaths you take, the movements you allow, and the moments you stop running and simply let your body be.

Because when the body feels safe, the heart follows. And when the heart feels safe, you stop surviving your emotions and start living them.

SEVENTEEN

---

# *Telling Yourself the Truth*

There comes a point in every journey where awareness isn't enough anymore. You know what hurts. You know what you've been avoiding. You've seen your patterns, your defenses, your fears. But knowing it and telling yourself the truth about it are two different things.

Awareness whispers. Truth speaks.

Awareness says, "I have a habit of shutting down when I'm uncomfortable." Truth says, "I'm afraid of being misunderstood, so I disappear first."

Awareness says, "I stay busy when I'm stressed." Truth says, "I stay busy because stillness forces me to feel."

Awareness opens the door. Truth walks through it.

For a long time, you might have mistaken self-awareness for healing. You could name your patterns, analyze your childhood, and talk about your emotions in detail, but still feel stuck. That's because insight without honesty doesn't change anything. You can't heal what you won't admit.

The kind of truth that heals is rarely dramatic. It's quiet. It's the kind that arrives late at night when the distractions fade. It's the honesty that sits in your chest before you find the words to say it out loud. It's not the kind of truth that demands to be performed; it's the kind that demands to be lived.

Telling yourself the truth is not about blaming yourself or anyone else. It's about clarity. It's about seeing things as they are, not as you wish they were. It's the moment you stop sugarcoating your pain and start meeting it directly. It's the moment you say, "This hurts," instead of "It's fine." It's the moment you say, "I'm scared," instead of "I'll figure it out." It's the moment you say, "I'm lonely," instead of "I'm just busy."

Truth is uncomfortable because it dismantles illusion. It exposes the ways you've been pretending. It reveals how often you've called avoidance peace and self-neglect strength. But discomfort isn't punishment. It's freedom beginning to take shape.

The reason truth feels heavy at first is because it breaks the agreements you've made with survival. Those agreements sound like, "If I stay quiet, things will stay calm," or "If I don't need too much, I won't be left," or "If I stay strong, no one will see me struggle." They once kept you safe. But now, they keep you from living.

When you tell yourself the truth, those old agreements lose power. You start to see that calm isn't the same as peace, that being needed isn't the same as being loved, that being in control isn't the same as being secure. The truth doesn't ruin your life. It realigns it.

Honesty with yourself will sometimes cost you comfort. It might mean admitting that certain relationships are no longer healthy. It might mean recognizing that your busyness is a form of avoidance. It might mean accepting that the person you've become is still healing from the person you had to be. But what honesty takes in comfort, it returns tenfold in peace.

It's tempting to delay truth until you feel ready. You tell yourself you'll deal with it later, that you'll be honest when things slow down. But avoidance doesn't protect you. It prolongs pain. The longer you delay truth, the heavier it becomes. The moment you name it, it begins to move.

You don't have to tell the whole truth at once. Start small. Tell yourself the truth about one thing. How you really feel about your job, your relationship, your habits, your exhaustion. Write it down if you need to. Say it out loud. Even if no one else hears it, you will. And that matters. Your body will feel the difference between silence and honesty.

Truth is a muscle. The more you use it, the stronger it gets. At first, it might tremble. You'll feel uncertain. But with practice, honesty starts to feel like relief. You no longer have to hold stories that aren't real. You no longer have to keep up appearances that exhaust you. You no longer have to explain away what your heart already knows.

And the more honest you become with yourself, the more peace you find with others. Relationships built on performance can't survive truth, but relationships built on truth don't need performance. The people who are meant for you will always respond better to honesty than perfection.

The truth will sometimes hurt, but it will never harm you. Lies harm. Pretending harms. Silence harms. Truth heals because it creates alignment between who you are and how you live. It gives your mind, body, and heart the same story to tell.

You don't need to have all the answers. You don't even need to know what comes next. You just need to start being honest with yourself about where you are. That's where transformation begins — not in control, but in clarity.

Because peace doesn't come from knowing everything will be okay. It comes from finally being real about what's not.

EIGHTEEN

---

# *Learning to Stay*

Every emotion has a lifespan. It rises, peaks, and passes. The problem is that most of us never let it complete that cycle. We either rush to escape it or drown in it. We distract ourselves or overthink it. We swing between suppression and obsession, never realizing that healing lives somewhere in the middle. That middle place is where you learn to stay.

Learning to stay doesn't mean liking what you feel. It means not running from it. It means giving your emotions enough space to speak before you silence them. It means being curious instead of critical, patient instead of panicked.

For most of your life, staying has probably felt dangerous. You were taught that feeling too deeply could make you weak or unstable. You might have learned that emotions are problems to solve, not experiences to move through. So when sadness shows up, you try to fix it. When anger rises, you try to suppress it. When anxiety hits, you try to outrun it. You spend your energy avoiding discomfort, not realizing that discomfort is where wisdom lives.

Avoidance feels like relief in the short term, but it keeps you disconnected in the long run. When you avoid what you feel, your emotions don't disappear; they just wait. They wait for the next quiet moment, the next pause, the next stillness. That's why certain feelings keep repeating. They aren't reminders of failure. They're reminders of what still needs your attention.

Learning to stay begins with recognizing that emotions are temporary. No feeling lasts forever. Every emotion, no matter how intense, eventually softens if you allow it to move through. What keeps emotions stuck is resistance - the effort to control, suppress, or rationalize them. When you stop resisting, the body and mind finally have room to process.

You can practice staying in simple ways. The next time you feel something uncomfortable, pause before reacting. Take a breath. Notice what's happening in your body. Is your chest tightening? Is your jaw clenching? Is your stomach tense? Just observe. You don't have to fix it. You don't have to label it right away. Simply notice and breathe.

At first, this will feel unnatural. Your nervous system is used to bracing, distracting, or escaping. Stillness will trigger the same alarms that used to keep you safe. That's okay. The goal isn't to stay perfectly calm. It's to stay present long enough for your body to learn that it can survive emotion without needing to shut down.

If you feel overwhelmed, you can ground yourself in the physical world. Focus on your senses. What do you see, hear, or feel around you? The present moment is the safest place you can be. Most emotional distress lives in the past or the future — in what already happened or what might happen. When you stay in the present, you step out of fear's timeline and back into your own.

Staying also means letting emotions move through without attaching to the stories that feed them. When sadness comes, notice it without telling yourself it will never end. When anger rises, feel it without turning it into self-criticism. When fear shows up, acknowledge it without predicting the worst. The more you separate emotion from narrative, the more freedom you find.

Over time, you begin to realize that emotions are not enemies to control but experiences to complete. Each one carries information, not identity. You are not your sadness, your anger, or your anxiety. You are the awareness behind them — the one who can sit with them, breathe through them, and choose your next step with clarity.

Learning to stay is also how you rebuild trust with yourself. Every time you remain present through discomfort, your body learns that you can handle it. That's how safety is restored — not through avoidance, but through endurance. You start to believe your own strength because you experience it, not just imagine it.

Eventually, you'll notice that emotions lose their power to overwhelm you. The storm still comes, but you no longer fear it. You understand its rhythm. You know that you can breathe, feel, and wait for it to pass. The more you stay, the faster it clears.

Staying doesn't mean getting stuck in pain. It means staying long enough to move through it. It means trusting that you can feel something fully without being consumed by it. It means learning that peace is not the absence of emotion, but the ability to stay steady within it.

You've spent most of your life running from discomfort, thinking that safety lived somewhere else — in control, in distraction, in performance. But safety isn't out there. It's here, in your ability to stay.

When you can sit in a moment of sadness without rushing to fix it, when you can feel anger without turning it inward, when you can face fear without retreating, that's when emotional maturity begins. That's when presence becomes peace.

Because the truth is simple: you don't heal by escaping your emotions. You heal by staying long enough to hear what they've been trying to say.

NINETEEN

---

# *The Practice of Peace*

Peace isn't something that just appears one day when everything finally calms down. It's something you practice, especially when things don't. It's the art of returning to center again and again, no matter what's happening around you. It's not control. It's connection to yourself, to the present moment, to what's real instead of what's imagined.

Most people think peace will come when the world slows down, when the to-do list is done, when everyone around them is happy, when the circumstances finally align. But peace doesn't live in perfect conditions. It lives in your ability to be still inside imperfect ones.

Peace is a discipline, not an accident. It's built through rhythm. It's formed through daily choices that create safety for your nervous system and honesty for your emotions. It's what happens when you stop chasing calm and start creating it.

You build peace the same way you build strength through repetition. You practice it when you wake up and take one deep breath before checking your phone. You practice it when you pause before reacting in frustration. You practice it when you take a walk instead of spiraling in thought. You practice it when you speak honestly instead of holding everything in.

These moments may seem small, but peace is made of small things. It's not a single decision. It's thousands of them, practiced quietly, consistently, and imperfectly.

One of the most powerful ways to cultivate peace is through presence. Presence means being here, not in your mind's version of what might go wrong or what already did. It means noticing the warmth of sunlight on your skin, the sound of your breath, the way your shoulders drop when you remember to relax. Presence brings you back to what's true that right now, in this moment, you are safe.

Another way to practice peace is through release. Let go of the constant need to solve what can't be solved right now. Some answers come only when you stop demanding them. Sometimes peace begins when you stop arguing with what is. Acceptance doesn't mean agreement. It means you've stopped fighting reality long enough to catch your breath.

Stillness is another form of practice. Not the forced kind that feels like doing nothing, but the kind that allows you to reset.

Sit quietly, close your eyes, and breathe. Let your body remember what it feels like to not be on guard. The world won't collapse because you paused. In fact, it might start to make more sense.

Movement is also part of peace. Not every calm moment is still. Sometimes peace lives in walking, stretching, cleaning, or creating. It's not about escaping the moment, but grounding yourself in it. The body holds the stories the mind can't, and movement gives those stories somewhere to go.

Boundaries are peace too. Every time you say no to something that drains you, you say yes to the calm you're trying to protect. Every time you limit what steals your energy — toxic people, endless scrolling, constant noise — you make room for what restores it.

Peace is not fragile. It's not something you lose the moment life gets hard. It's something you learn to return to. The more you practice, the faster you find your way back. Some days it might take a breath. Other days it might take a long walk or a good cry. But peace is always within reach because it lives inside you, not around you.

Practicing peace doesn't mean avoiding emotion. It means meeting emotion with gentleness. When sadness comes, peace says, "You can stay here until you're ready to go." When anger comes, peace says, "I can feel you without letting you take over." When joy comes, peace says, "I'm safe enough to let you in."

Peace doesn't erase emotion; it balances it. It reminds you that you are not what you feel, you are the one feeling it. It reminds you that chaos outside of you doesn't have to create chaos within you.

The more you practice peace, the more your body begins to trust it. The same way it once learned to expect stress, it can learn to expect calm. That's how healing happens, not in one big breakthrough, but in quiet repetition.

Over time, peace becomes your default instead of your goal. It becomes the atmosphere you live in, not the thing you chase. You stop needing the world to behave before you can breathe. You start realizing that your calm isn't a reward for good circumstances; it's a choice you make in the middle of them.

The practice of peace is simple, but it isn't easy. It asks you to slow down in a world that glorifies urgency. It asks you to listen to your body when your mind wants to keep moving. It asks you to surrender control and trust that calm is stronger than chaos.

But the more you practice, the more natural it becomes. Peace stops being something you visit and starts being where you live.

And once you know how to live there, nothing external can take it from you.

TWENTY

---

# *Becoming the Anchor*

Once you learn how to stay present through your own emotions, something begins to shift. The calm that used to feel out of reach starts to live inside you. You find yourself reacting less and listening more. You notice that peace isn't something you visit anymore; it's something you carry. And as that happens, you start to become something new, an anchor.

An anchor doesn't stop the waves. It holds steady while the water moves. That's what emotional maturity feels like. It doesn't mean life stops being difficult. It means difficulty no longer knocks you off course. You still feel everything, but you're not defined by it. You can meet joy without losing focus and meet pain without losing yourself.

Most people think leadership — whether in families, friendships, or work — comes from authority or achievement. But real leadership begins with regulation. When you are steady, the people around you feel safe. When you are calm, they relax. When you listen instead of react, you create space for others to come back to themselves.

Becoming an anchor isn't about being perfect or emotionless. It's about being grounded enough to handle your emotions without projecting them. It's about being able to say, "I'm upset," without turning that upset into destruction. It's about staying centered in truth, even when others are caught in fear.

You may not realize how powerful your presence becomes when you are at peace. The same way anxiety is contagious, so is calm. People feel it before they understand it. They notice that conversations around you feel safer. They find themselves breathing easier in your company. They may not know why, but it's because your nervous system is no longer feeding theirs chaos. It's offering stability.

This is what happens when healing moves from the personal to the relational. Your peace starts to teach others what safety feels like. Your honesty makes it easier for them to be honest. Your boundaries show them what respect looks like. Your stillness reminds them that they can slow down too.

But being the anchor doesn't mean you take responsibility for everyone else's emotions. That's the trap many fall back into. Mistaking steadiness for saviorhood. You can hold space for others without holding their pain. You can offer calm without carrying their chaos. The goal is not to fix. It's to stay grounded so that others can find their own footing.

There will still be days when you wobble. You'll get triggered, lose your patience, or feel overwhelmed. Anchors aren't unmovable; they're secure enough to return to center. The practice is not perfection. It's return. You notice when you drift and you come back to breath, to presence, to truth.

Becoming an anchor also changes the way you love. You stop needing people to regulate you. You stop expecting them to save you from discomfort. You begin to meet relationships from stability instead of need. You can be close without clinging, available without overextending, kind without losing boundaries. You start to experience love that feels peaceful instead of performative.

And the most beautiful part is that your peace starts to multiply. The steadier you become, the more permission others feel to be honest, gentle, and patient too. You become proof that calm isn't passive, that softness isn't weakness, that peace isn't the absence of feeling. It's the full expression of it, held with grace.

You will still feel deeply. You will still have moments of frustration, sadness, and fear. But instead of being swept away, you'll know how to stand in the middle of it and stay. That's the power of an anchor. It doesn't stop the storm. It makes it survivable.

When you become the anchor, you realize that leadership doesn't start with influence. It starts with presence. It starts with knowing yourself so deeply that your steadiness becomes a gift to others. You don't have to say much. You don't have to convince anyone. You simply have to be.

And in being, you remind others that peace is possible.

That is what it means to show up emotionally. Not just for yourself, but for the world around you.

TWENTY-ONE

---

# *The Confidence to Trust Yourself*

Confidence isn't something you find. It's something you build.

For years, you might have looked at confident people and wondered what they had that you didn't. Maybe you thought it was personality, upbringing, or luck. But real confidence doesn't come from external approval. It comes from integrity. The quiet alignment between what you say and what you do.

Confidence grows every time you keep a promise to yourself.

Most people lose trust in themselves the same way relationships fall apart, slowly, through small betrayals that seem harmless at the time. You say you'll rest, but you keep working. You say you'll speak up, but you stay quiet. You say you'll stop tolerating something, but you keep letting it slide. Each time you break your own word, you teach yourself that you can't be counted on. You create a split inside, one part that hopes and one part that doubts.

Over time, that doubt becomes louder than your intentions. You stop believing in your own follow-through. You start to hesitate before making commitments because you've learned, unconsciously, that you don't keep them. That's where insecurity comes from. Not a lack of ability, but a lack of trust in your own consistency.

When you start keeping promises to yourself, something powerful shifts. The voice of doubt softens. The part of you that used to say, "You won't follow through," starts to quiet. You begin to feel steady. Grounded. Clear. Confidence stops being something you have to perform. It becomes something you live.

This is why self-discipline and emotional health are inseparable. Discipline isn't punishment. It's self-respect. It's saying, "I matter enough to do what I said I would." It's showing up for yourself the same way you've always shown up for others.

The promises don't have to be grand. They just have to be kept. Small, consistent integrity is what builds trust. When you say you'll take a walk and you do, your body learns to believe you. When you say you'll take a break and actually rest, your nervous system learns that you mean it. When you say you'll tell the truth and follow through, your mind starts to relax into alignment.

You don't build confidence through perfection. You build it through repair. You'll still miss the mark sometimes. You'll still fall short. But every time you notice it and return to honesty, you prove that you're reliable. You show yourself that failure doesn't erase integrity. It refines it.

Confidence doesn't come from never doubting yourself. It comes from knowing how to move through doubt without abandoning yourself. It's not the loud certainty that nothing will go wrong. It's the quiet assurance that even if it does, you'll handle it with grace.

This kind of confidence doesn't need an audience. It doesn't shout or demand attention. It doesn't depend on anyone else believing in you. It comes from the inside out, from the peace that grows when your words, actions, and values finally match.

Keeping promises to yourself is an act of love. It's how you rebuild safety from the inside. It's how you teach your body and your mind that you can be trusted again. It's how you create a relationship with yourself that feels reliable. One where honesty replaces guilt and follow-through replaces shame.

If you've spent most of your life keeping promises to others and breaking them with yourself, it will take time to rebuild. Start small. Pick one thing each day that matters and honor it fully. When you say you'll take a moment to breathe, do it. When you say you'll go for a walk, follow through. When you say you'll be kind to yourself, keep that promise like your peace depends on it because it does.

Confidence is not a reward for success. It's the result of alignment. It's knowing that your word means something. It's being able to look at yourself at the end of the day and say, "I did what I said I would."

And the more you do that, the stronger the trust becomes.

Eventually, you stop questioning whether you're capable. You stop overexplaining yourself. You stop looking for validation. You carry quiet assurance, the kind that doesn't need to be proven.

Because confidence isn't about never falling short. It's about knowing that when you do, you'll get back up. Not out of pressure, but out of trust.

And when you live that way, you no longer have to convince anyone else that you're confident. You just are.

TWENTY-TWO

---

# *What Healing Isn't*

Healing has become a word that's easy to say but hard to live. It's talked about everywhere — online, in books, in conversations with friends — yet so often misunderstood. Somewhere along the way, healing started to sound like a destination, like something you arrive at once you've done enough work. But healing isn't a finish line. It's a way of living.

It's important to understand what healing is not, because without that clarity, you can spend years chasing the wrong kind of peace.

Healing isn't about feeling good all the time. It's about learning to feel honestly. Sometimes healing hurts. Sometimes it's confusing. Sometimes it looks like sitting in silence with emotions you used to run from. The absence of pain doesn't mean you're healed. It just means you're numb. True healing teaches you how to stay grounded when the pain comes back.

Healing isn't constant progress. It moves in waves. Some days you'll feel light and clear. Other days you'll feel like you've gone backward. You haven't. The path just loops. Every time you revisit an old pattern with more awareness, you're not failing. You're deepening.

Healing isn't about fixing your emotions. It's about understanding them. The goal isn't to never feel anger, sadness, or fear again. It's to stop being ruled by them. Emotional peace doesn't mean never getting upset. It means knowing what to do when you do.

Healing isn't about control. It's about trust. The more you try to micromanage your inner world, the more anxious you'll become. You can't schedule your growth or rush your release. Healing happens in its own time, through moments of honesty, grace, and surrender.

Healing isn't about perfection. You won't always respond calmly. You won't always get your boundaries right. You won't always feel strong. And that's okay. Perfectionism is just another disguise for fear. Real healing comes with self-compassion. The kind that says, "Even when I mess up, I'm still learning."

Healing isn't self-absorption. It's self-responsibility. It's not about dissecting every emotion or centering every conversation on your pain. It's about owning your patterns and choosing to grow through them. Healing doesn't mean blaming others endlessly. It means recognizing how you've adapted and deciding what you want to carry forward.

Healing isn't detachment. It's engagement. It's not about becoming so "zen" that nothing affects you. It's about being so grounded that you can stay connected to life, even when it challenges you. You don't rise above your emotions; you learn to live beside them.

Healing isn't isolation. Growth doesn't require you to do it all alone. It's built through connection, honesty, and support. You were wounded in relationships, and much of your healing will happen in relationships too. The kind that honor truth and safety instead of performance and perfection.

Healing isn't about being unbothered. It's about being available to yourself, to others, to the full experience of being alive. It's the opposite of apathy. It's awareness. It's feeling everything without losing yourself in it.

Healing isn't a brand, a trend, or a performance. It's not something to prove online. It's not aesthetic. It's real work. It's crying in parking lots. It's apologizing when you're wrong. It's learning to rest before you burn out. It's setting boundaries that disappoint people you love. It's forgiving yourself a hundred times a day.

Healing isn't about who you were before the pain. It's about who you become after it. You can't go back, but you can go forward. softer, wiser, more grounded, and more at peace.

And finally, healing isn't something you do once. It's something you practice. It's how you breathe, rest, listen, and tell the truth. It's how you respond when life tests you. It's how you come home to yourself again and again.

You don't need to be perfect to be healing. You just need to stay honest. You don't need to be calm all the time to be growing. You just need to keep showing up.

Healing isn't an image. It's a rhythm. It's not what you show others. It's how you treat yourself when no one is watching.

That's where peace begins. Not in perfection, but in presence.

TWENTY-THREE

---

# *Be the Light, Not the Lesson*

The moment awareness clicks, it can feel like everything changes at once. You start to see patterns you never noticed before, in yourself, in your relationships, in the people you love. You recognize where pain has been passed down and where avoidance has disguised itself as peace. The clarity feels like power. For a while, it almost feels like awakening.

But awareness without restraint can turn into judgment.

It's easy to look around and want everyone else to see what you see. You notice the same patterns in others that you've been working so hard to break in yourself. You can feel the old dynamics repeating. And because you care, you want to help them understand. You want to save them from the pain you've already lived through.

That instinct comes from compassion, but it can easily turn into control. You start explaining, correcting, or pushing your insight onto people who didn't ask for it. You think you're showing them love, but what they feel is pressure. Healing that was meant to bring connection starts creating distance.

The truth is that no one can be forced into awareness. People don't wake up because someone tells them to. They wake up when they are ready. When life brings them to that moment of stillness or pain or revelation that makes them finally open their eyes.

Your job isn't to rush their process. It's to respect it.

Emotional maturity means learning the difference between understanding and wisdom. Understanding sees what's happening. Wisdom knows when to speak and when to stay silent. Understanding wants to fix. Wisdom knows that presence often heals more than words ever could.

You can't lead someone into growth by pointing out what they can't yet see. You lead them by living what you've learned so clearly that your peace becomes the proof. You show them what healing looks like, not by explaining it, but by embodying it.

There's a quiet power in being steady while others are still searching. It's not passive. It's patient. It's the kind of strength that allows people to feel safe enough to question themselves. You don't have to push them toward awareness. You just have to stay rooted in your own.

When you're truly at peace, you stop needing everyone else to understand you. You stop trying to convince, correct, or convert. You trust that your light will speak for itself. People may not recognize it right away, but they'll feel it. And when they're ready, they'll remember how it felt to be near it.

That's what real emotional intelligence looks like. It's not the need to prove you've grown. It's the ability to stay kind when others haven't yet. It's being grounded enough to love people through their process without needing to manage it. It's knowing that compassion doesn't always mean involvement. Sometimes it means quiet faith that they'll find their own way.

So when you start to see clearly, resist the urge to teach everyone what you've learned. Let your calm be the example. Let your boundaries be the lesson. Let your presence be the proof.

Be the light, not the lesson.

Because light doesn't convince anyone to see. It simply shines. Until others are ready to open their eyes.

TWENTY-FOUR

---

# *Fully Here*

There comes a moment in every healing journey when you realize there's nothing left to fix. Not because everything is perfect, but because you've stopped needing it to be. The striving quiets. The guilt softens. The constant effort to hold everything together begins to fade. What takes its place isn't excitement or relief, it's something deeper. It's peace.

Being fully here doesn't mean you never feel pain again. It means pain no longer defines you. It means emotions can move through you without taking over. It means you can face life as it is. The joy, the loss, the change, the beauty, and remain whole.

For a long time, you probably thought emotional control was the goal. You wanted to master your feelings, to stay calm no matter what. But control was never the answer. Connection was. The work was never about tightening your grip. It was about softening it. It was about remembering that your emotions aren't problems to solve; they're experiences to meet.

When you finally start living this way, everything begins to feel different. You listen more than you explain. You breathe before you react. You rest before you break. You stop chasing moments of peace and start building a life that holds it naturally.

You begin to understand that peace doesn't mean nothing ever hurts. It means you trust yourself to move through whatever does. You stop fearing emotion because you've learned that you can handle it. You've proven to yourself that feeling isn't weakness; it's aliveness.

Being fully here means you've stopped running, from your emotions, from your past, from yourself. It means you can sit in a quiet room and not feel the need to fill it. It means you can feel sadness without spiraling and joy without waiting for it to disappear. It means you can tell the truth about how you feel without apology or performance.

Presence becomes your new form of power. You stop needing to predict the future because you're finally living the moment you're in. You stop replaying the past because you've already learned from it. You realize that life isn't waiting for you somewhere else. It's happening now, right here, in every breath, every sensation, every heartbeat.

You start to notice the small things again. The warmth of sunlight on your face. The laughter that comes without effort. The quiet satisfaction of being able to exhale without tension. These are not small moments. They're proof of healing. They're evidence that you've come home to yourself.

You no longer chase strength. You embody it. You no longer chase calm. You create it. You no longer chase love. You become it. That's what showing up emotionally really means to live awake, honest, and open, even when it would be easier to shut down.

The world will keep moving. People will still disappoint you. Life will still surprise you. But none of it will pull you away from yourself anymore. You've built something solid inside, a foundation of honesty, awareness, and peace. You can trust it. You can trust you.

You'll still have days where you stumble back into old habits. You'll still have moments when "I'm fine" slips out of your mouth before you even think. That's okay. The difference now is that you'll notice it. You'll pause. You'll take a breath and return to truth. Healing isn't about never falling back. It's about always finding your way home.

Being fully here means you've made peace with being human. It means you've stopped performing and started living. It means you finally understand that wholeness was never about perfection. It was about presence.

You are not your pain. You are not your past. You are not your patterns. You are the one who lived through them, learned from them, and kept showing up anyway.

And that's what it means to show up more emotionally. To be fully here.

To feel. To stay. To live.

TWENTY-FIVE

---

# *When You Remember Yourself*

At the beginning of this book, you were probably tired. Not just the kind of tired that sleep fixes, but the kind that settles in your soul. You had been carrying yourself through life on strength and responsibility, trying to keep everything steady while quietly feeling disconnected from it all.

Maybe you didn't have the words for what you were feeling. You just knew something was missing. You were functioning, but not fully living. You were present, but not really here.

Now, after walking through these pages, you've learned something simple but profound. That your emotions were never the enemy. They were the way home.

Every moment of awareness, every pause to breathe, every truth you let surface has been a form of coming back to yourself. You have learned to see your emotions not as problems to fix, but as messages to honor. You've begun to understand that healing doesn't look like perfection. It looks like honesty. It looks like softness. It looks like remembering that you were never broken, just disconnected.

You may not feel completely healed yet, and that's okay. Healing isn't a finish line. It's a rhythm, a returning. Every time you stop running from what you feel, every time you tell yourself the truth, every time you choose calm over control, you are practicing what it means to live whole.

You will still have hard days. You will still be tempted to shut down, to stay busy, to avoid what hurts. But the difference now is that you know what's happening. You can see it. You can meet it with compassion instead of judgment. And that awareness changes everything.

This is the gift of showing up emotionally. You no longer need to numb your way through life or perform strength to feel safe. You can feel fully and remain steady. You can be vulnerable and still be strong. You can love deeply and still stay grounded.

When you live this way, the world begins to look different. Colors seem brighter. Conversations feel deeper. Ordinary moments become sacred because you're actually in them. You're no longer watching your life from a distance. You're living it from within.

Being fully human means you will always feel, joy, grief, frustration, hope, all of it. But now you understand that emotions aren't obstacles to peace. They are paths to it. They are how your soul speaks. They are how you stay connected to life.

You've spent so much time trying to be enough. What you've discovered is that you always were. You just needed to stop performing long enough to remember it.

So take a breath. Feel it move through you.

You're here.

You made it back.

And from here forward, you don't have to live half-alive anymore. You know how to stay. You know how to listen. You know how to be fully, beautifully, humanly here.

That's what it means to show up more emotionally.

To remember yourself. And to never leave again.

TWENTY-SIX

---

# *Emotion Index*

## How to Use This Section

This part of the book is meant to be a companion, not a lecture. It's here for the moments when you feel something and don't know what to do with it. Maybe it's anger that keeps showing up in the same conversations. Maybe it's sadness you can't explain. Maybe you're just tired of feeling everything all the time.

You don't have to read this section straight through. Think of it as a guide you can return to whenever an emotion feels too big, too confusing, or too familiar. Each chapter names what the emotion often looks like in everyday life, where it usually comes from, and what to do when it shows up.

Emotions are messengers. They're not problems to fix or proof that you're broken. They're signals that something inside you needs attention: a need, a memory, a boundary, or a truth that hasn't been heard.

When you understand what an emotion is trying to tell you, it loses its power to control you. That's the point of this section: not to make your emotions disappear, but to help you *understand* them so you can respond with clarity instead of reaction.

Here's how to use what follows:

- **Find yourself.** Start with the emotion that feels closest to what you're feeling. You might see yourself in more than one. That's normal.

- **Read slowly.** Let the words land. The goal isn't to rush through, but to recognize what feels true.

- **Reflect gently.** When something hits home, pause and ask, "Where have I felt this before?" Emotions repeat until they're understood.

- **Return often.** Healing isn't a one-time read. It's a relationship with yourself. Come back to these pages whenever you need to remember that your feelings make sense — and that you have the tools to move through them.

You don't have to fear your emotions anymore. Once you learn to listen to them, you'll realize they've been trying to help you all along.

\*\*\*

# Abandonment

## Where You're At

You feel abandonment when someone you needed wasn't there — physically, emotionally, or both. It's that deep ache that says, "I can't rely on anyone to stay." Sometimes it comes from a clear moment, like being left, ignored, or replaced. Other times it's subtle, the slow erosion of trust as people drift away, stop listening, or fail to show up when you need them most.

Abandonment doesn't just hurt in the moment. It leaves a mark. It teaches you to expect loss, to stay guarded, to leave before you can be left. Even now, when someone pulls away or takes too long to respond, that same old feeling wakes up inside you — the fear that you're about to be alone again.

You might tell yourself you're fine with independence, that you don't need anyone. But underneath that strength is often a quiet longing to feel safe in someone's presence and to finally believe they won't leave.

## What's Beneath It

Feeling abandoned usually starts in childhood, when the people who were supposed to make you feel safe couldn't.

Maybe they were absent, distracted, or inconsistent. Maybe love felt temporary or earned. When connection isn't reliable early on, your nervous system learns that closeness equals risk.

As an adult, this can show up in two extremes. You either cling tightly to people, afraid they'll disappear, or you keep your distance to avoid being hurt again. Both are ways of trying to protect yourself from the pain of loss.

But abandonment isn't always about someone leaving. It can also come from being emotionally unseen. You can be in a room full of people — even loved ones — and still feel alone if you can't be yourself there.

**What It Might Look Like**

- You fear people will leave once they really know you.

- You overgive in relationships to keep people close.

- You feel anxious when someone doesn't text back or changes plans.

- You leave situations first to avoid being left.

- You struggle to fully trust, even when people show consistency.

**How to Work Through It**

Start by acknowledging the wound without judging it. It makes sense that you fear being left — you've lived through loss. You're not needy; you're remembering.

Then, remind yourself that the people who left before aren't everyone. The pain was real, but it doesn't define what all connection must be. Begin testing that belief with small acts of trust. Let someone help you with something minor. Share a thought you'd normally keep to yourself. Let the world prove that not everyone disappears.

If you find yourself pulling away when things get close, pause. Ask, "Am I protecting myself from what's happening now, or from what happened then?" Most of the time, it's the past speaking. Awareness gives you the power to choose a different response.

Learn to give yourself the safety others couldn't. That means keeping your promises to yourself, meeting your own needs first, and being present when emotions rise. When you become your own safe place, the fear of being left begins to lose its grip.

**What to Remember**

Feeling abandoned doesn't mean you're unlovable. It means someone else's absence taught you to doubt what was always true — that you are worthy of love that stays.

You can't rewrite who left, but you can redefine what love means now. It doesn't have to look like survival anymore. It can look like peace, steadiness, and choice.

Abandonment may have shaped you, but it doesn't have to guide you. The more you learn to stay with yourself — through fear, through loneliness, through pain — the less power anyone else's leaving will ever have.

# Anger

**Where You're At**

You feel anger when something feels unfair, disrespectful, or out of your control. It rises fast — heat in your chest, tightness in your jaw, the urge to shout, argue, or walk away. It can feel like energy that has nowhere to go.

Anger isn't always loud. Sometimes it shows up quietly — through irritability, sarcasm, or a short fuse over small things. You tell yourself you're "fine," but inside, you're carrying years of swallowed frustration. Maybe it's toward someone who hurt you and never apologized. Maybe it's toward yourself for staying silent.

Anger doesn't make you a bad person. It's proof that something inside you still believes you deserve better.

**What's Beneath It**

Feeling anger is often a sign that your boundaries have been crossed or your needs ignored. Many of us grew up learning that anger was dangerous — that it caused conflict or disappointment. So we buried it, thinking that staying calm made us strong. But suppressed anger doesn't disappear. It turns into resentment, exhaustion, or shame.

Sometimes, anger shows up to protect softer emotions like hurt or sadness. When you didn't feel safe enough to express pain, anger became the bodyguard for your heart. It kept you from feeling powerless. It gave you energy when everything else felt numb.

The key isn't to get rid of anger. It's to learn what it's trying to tell you before it turns into destruction.

**What It Might Look Like**

- You snap at small things because you're holding onto bigger ones.

- You replay arguments in your head, thinking about what you wish you'd said.

- You take on too much, then explode when no one notices.

- You avoid people who constantly drain you but feel guilty for doing it.

- You feel tense or restless even when no one's doing anything wrong.

**How to Work Through It**

Start by acknowledging the feeling without shaming yourself
for it. Say, "I feel angry right now." Don't say, "I am angry."
The difference matters. One is a state; the other is an
identity.

Then ask, "What's the story underneath this feeling?" Anger is
often protecting something — disappointment, hurt, fear, or
the exhaustion of always being the strong one. Once you know
what's underneath, you can address the real issue instead of
fighting the symptom.

Give anger a healthy outlet. Move your body. Go for a walk, hit
a pillow, shout in the car, write without editing. Anger is
energy. It needs somewhere to go, not someone to hurt.

If anger shows up often, pay attention to your boundaries.
Who or what are you saying yes to when you really mean no?
Anger grows in silence. Every time you speak your truth
calmly and clearly, it loses power.

You don't have to suppress it, and you don't have to act it out.
You can learn to listen to it, then release it.

**What to Remember**

Feeling anger doesn't make you bad or broken. It means a part
of you is still fighting for fairness, honesty, and respect.
That's not something to be ashamed of — that's strength in
disguise.

Your job isn't to avoid anger. It's to guide it. Let it show you where you need to set boundaries, speak up, or finally let go. When anger becomes a teacher instead of a weapon, it stops burning you from the inside out and starts lighting the way forward.

# Anxiety

**Where You're At**

You feel anxious when your body believes something bad is about to happen, even if you can't see what it is. Your chest tightens. Your thoughts speed up. Your heart beats harder, as if it's trying to keep you safe by staying ahead of whatever might go wrong. You might lie awake at night thinking through every possible scenario, or replaying every conversation, trying to find the moment you could have done something differently. It's exhausting.

This feeling doesn't mean you're broken. It means your body is trying to protect you. For a long time, staying alert probably helped you survive — it kept you ready, aware, careful. But the problem is that now, even when you're safe, your body hasn't learned that yet.

**What's Beneath It**

Feeling anxious usually comes from living in an environment that felt unpredictable. Maybe peace never lasted long. Maybe love and anger showed up in the same voice. Maybe you had to read moods like warning signs. You learned to stay prepared for whatever came next because you couldn't rely on calm to last. That's not weakness. It's adaptation.

Over time, your mind and body linked "being alert" with "being safe." And now, years later, they still think calm means danger — because calm was the moment before things fell apart. Anxiety isn't a flaw. It's your body's way of trying to make sure you never get caught off guard again.

**What It Might Look Like**

- You plan every detail of your day, not out of joy, but out of fear that something will go wrong if you don't.

- You replay what you said to someone, trying to figure out if you offended them.

- You stay constantly busy because slowing down feels risky.

- You feel tension in your shoulders or stomach even on days that seem fine.

- You get irritable or distracted when there's "nothing wrong," because stillness makes your body uneasy.

**How to Work Through It**

The first step is to notice it without judgment. Instead of saying "I am anxious," say "I feel anxious right now." That small change matters. It reminds you that feelings pass — they don't define you.

Next, remind your body that it's safe to stand down. Take one slow breath in through your nose, then let it out through your mouth longer than you took it in. Do that again, slower this time. Let your shoulders drop. Let your tongue rest at the bottom of your mouth. Look around and name three things you can see, two things you can touch, and one sound you can hear. This brings you out of the future and back into the present.

If your mind keeps racing, grab a notebook and write down what it's trying to solve. Don't try to fix it — just empty it. Writing helps your brain separate real problems from imagined ones. Once you see them clearly, they lose their power.

When you start to feel anxious again — and you will — see it as a signal, not a setback. Your body is trying to keep you safe the only way it knows how. Instead of fighting it, say thank you. Then show it that safety doesn't come from control. It comes from presence.

**What to Remember**

Feeling anxious doesn't mean something's wrong with you. It means your body learned to care deeply about safety. That awareness kept you alive, but now you get to teach it something new — that calm doesn't mean danger, and peace doesn't mean weakness.

You don't have to control everything to be safe. You just have to come back to this moment, again and again, until your body finally believes you're okay. And one day, it will.

# Control

**Where You're At**

You feel the need for control when uncertainty starts to feel unsafe. You make plans, set routines, double-check details, and try to keep everything in order — not because you enjoy it, but because it helps you breathe. You tell yourself that as long as things go according to plan, everything will be fine.

But control is exhausting. It keeps your mind constantly working, trying to manage every possible outcome. It tricks you into believing that peace will come once everything is handled perfectly — but perfection keeps moving just out of reach.

You might call it responsibility or leadership, but underneath it is fear. Fear that if you stop holding it all together, everything — or everyone — might fall apart.

**What's Beneath It**

Feeling the need for control usually comes from a time when life felt unpredictable or unsafe. Maybe you grew up in chaos, where peace never lasted long. Maybe you learned that staying ahead of problems was the only way to avoid being hurt or disappointed. Control became your safety net.

At its core, control is about protection — not power. It's an attempt to create order in a world that once felt threatening. But over time, that same protection starts to cost you peace. You stop trusting life. You stop trusting people. You even stop trusting yourself to handle uncertainty.

Control feels safe, but it often keeps you trapped in vigilance instead of freedom.

**What It Might Look Like**

- You get anxious when plans change or things don't go your way.

- You micromanage situations or people to avoid surprises.

- You replay conversations, trying to make sense of what went wrong.

- You struggle to rest because something always feels unfinished.

- You feel responsible for everyone's comfort and outcomes.

**How to Work Through It**

Start by acknowledging the truth — control helped you survive. It made you reliable, organized, and capable. You don't need to hate that part of yourself. You just need to help it rest.

When you feel the urge to tighten your grip, pause and ask, "What am I afraid will happen if I let this go?" Usually, the answer isn't about the situation — it's about the fear of losing safety, love, or approval. Naming that fear brings you back to reality.

Next, practice releasing control in small ways. Let someone else make a decision, even if you'd do it differently. Skip your routine for one day. Sit in silence without filling it. Each small act of surrender teaches your nervous system that the world won't collapse without your constant supervision.

Remind yourself that control doesn't create safety — *trust* does. And trust grows when you let life unfold and discover that you can handle what comes. The more evidence you gather that you're safe even when things go off-plan, the easier it becomes to relax.

**What to Remember**

Wanting control doesn't make you obsessive or difficult. It makes you human — someone who learned to survive uncertainty by staying alert.

You don't have to let go of structure or responsibility to find peace. You just have to release the illusion that peace only exists when everything is perfect.

True control isn't about managing every detail. It's about knowing that whatever happens, you'll still be okay. You've survived far worse than a plan that didn't work out. You can trust yourself now — not because you can predict everything, but because you can handle anything.

# Defensiveness

### Where You're At

You feel defensive when something inside you senses attack, even if no one meant harm. Your chest tightens, your jaw sets, and before you know it, you're explaining, justifying, or shutting down. Sometimes you argue; other times, you withdraw completely. You want to be understood, not blamed.

Defensiveness often comes from feeling misunderstood or unseen. It's that urge to say, "That's not what I meant," or "You don't know the whole story." Deep down, you're trying to protect something tender — your intentions, your worth, your goodness.

You're not trying to win a fight. You're trying to stop the feeling of being wrong about who you are.

### What's Beneath It

Feeling defensive is often rooted in experiences where being wrong wasn't safe. Maybe mistakes were punished instead of understood. Maybe criticism meant rejection. Maybe you had to be right to be respected. Over time, you learned to see correction as danger, not dialogue.

Defensiveness forms as a shield. It keeps you from feeling small, ashamed, or exposed. The problem is that it also keeps love and growth from getting close. When you're busy protecting your image, you can't receive understanding — even when it's being offered.

Underneath defensiveness is usually fear: fear of being misunderstood, of disappointing others, or of being seen as less than good. That fear deserves compassion, not judgment.

**What It Might Look Like**

- You explain yourself right away when someone gives feedback.

- You get tense or argumentative during disagreements.

- You avoid conversations that might lead to conflict.

- You feel the need to prove your intentions, even when no one asked.

- You take neutral comments personally or feel easily misunderstood.

**How to Work Through It**

The first step is to pause before reacting. Take a breath and ask, "Do I feel attacked, or do I just feel exposed?" Sometimes what feels like an attack is actually discomfort. You're not being threatened — you're being seen.

Next, remind yourself that being wrong or misunderstood doesn't make you unworthy. It just makes you human. You don't need to defend your goodness; it's already there.

When someone offers feedback, try to listen for what's true instead of listening for what hurts. You don't have to agree with everything. Just stay open long enough to decide calmly what feels fair and what doesn't.

If defensiveness shows up mid-conversation, slow down. You can always say, "I need a moment to think about that." Giving yourself space helps your nervous system settle so you can respond, not react.

And if you do get defensive, that's okay too. It's an old reflex, not a failure. The goal isn't to never feel it — it's to notice it sooner and choose differently.

**What to Remember**

Feeling defensive doesn't mean you're prideful or closed-minded. It means you're protecting a part of yourself that once got hurt when it tried to be open.

You don't have to guard yourself from everyone. You can handle disagreement without losing dignity. You can hear truth without losing self-respect.

Defensiveness loosens its grip when you realize you don't
have to fight to prove your worth — you only have to
remember it.

# Disappointment

**Where You're At**

You feel disappointment when life doesn't meet your
expectations — when something or someone you hoped for
doesn't turn out the way you imagined. It's the sinking feeling
that comes after you gave your best, waited patiently, or
believed deeply, only to end up holding less than you thought
you would.

Sometimes it's sharp and specific, like a lost opportunity or a
promise broken. Other times it's quieter — the slow
realization that something you've been working toward just
isn't going to happen. You might tell yourself to move on, but
the heaviness stays. It's not just about what you didn't get —
it's about what that moment meant to you.

Disappointment can make you doubt your effort, your
intuition, even your hope. But it's not a sign that you were
wrong to care. It's a sign that you were brave enough to
believe.

**What's Beneath It**

Feeling disappointed usually comes from attachment — from investing your time, energy, and heart into something that mattered. You built an expectation around it, whether it was a person, a plan, or a version of your future. And when it didn't work out, it left a gap where your hope used to be.

Maybe you grew up in an environment where expectations were rarely met, so disappointment feels familiar — like an old ache you've learned to live with. Or maybe you learned that hoping too much only leads to pain, so now you protect yourself by lowering the bar. But doing that also keeps you from experiencing joy when things *do* work out.

Disappointment isn't failure. It's the emotional bruise left by caring deeply in a world that doesn't always cooperate.

**What It Might Look Like**

- You feel detached or numb after a setback, pretending it doesn't matter.

- You replay what happened, wondering what you could've done differently.

- You lose motivation or avoid trying again because you don't want to be let down.

- You say things like "I should've known better" to protect yourself from hope.

- You struggle to trust people or opportunities because you don't want to be hurt again.

**How to Work Through It**

Start by letting yourself feel it. You don't have to minimize the pain to move on. It's okay to admit that you're hurt or that you wish things were different. Disappointment lingers when it's denied.

Then, name what the disappointment actually took from you. Was it your confidence? Your sense of safety? Your belief in fairness? Once you identify what you lost, you can begin to rebuild it.

Give yourself permission to grieve. Grief isn't just for death — it's for the loss of expectations too. Sit with the ache instead of rushing to replace it. Write down what you hoped would happen and what it meant to you. Honor it.

When you're ready, look for what the experience taught you about yourself. Maybe it revealed how deeply you care, how resilient you are, or how much more you deserve. Disappointment can be a mirror that reflects your capacity for hope, not the end of it.

Finally, take one small step toward trying again — not because you're sure it will work, but because your heart deserves to stay open. Each new attempt is a quiet act of courage.

**What to Remember**

Feeling disappointed doesn't mean you were foolish to hope. It means you cared enough to imagine something better.

You don't have to harden yourself to avoid being let down again. You just have to trust that you can recover when it happens.

Disappointment is a sign that your heart still believes in more. And while it hurts to fall short, the fact that you're still willing to care means you haven't given up on life — and that's what will carry you forward.

# Fear

### Where You're At

You feel fear when something inside you whispers that you might not be safe, even if your life looks perfectly fine on the outside. It's that cold feeling in your stomach before a difficult conversation, the hesitation before saying what you really think, or the quiet panic that hits you when life changes and you can't control the outcome.

Fear doesn't always scream. Sometimes it hides in your planning, your politeness, or your perfectionism. It can sound like "I'm just being careful" when what you really mean is "I'm scared of what will happen if I'm not."

You might not even call it fear anymore. You might call it stress, pressure, responsibility, or being realistic. But underneath all those words is the same thing — the need to feel safe.

## What's Beneath It

Feeling fear is natural. It's how your body tries to protect you from harm. But when you've lived through situations that made you feel unsafe — emotionally, physically, or relationally — your body can start to confuse *familiar* with *safe*.

If you grew up in a home where love was unpredictable, or where mistakes came with consequences, your body learned that staying small, quiet, or agreeable was the best way to survive. Fear taught you how to read danger, even when it wasn't spoken out loud. It kept you alert. It made you observant. It helped you survive.

The problem is, now it's showing up in moments that don't require that same level of protection. Your mind still assumes that risk equals danger, so you pull back, overthink, or freeze when life invites you forward.

## What It Might Look Like

- You stay in jobs, relationships, or routines that don't feel right because they feel predictable.

- You downplay your dreams or talk yourself out of trying new things.

- You keep quiet to avoid conflict, even when something hurts you.

- You second-guess your intuition because you've learned to distrust it.

- You make choices that protect you from rejection instead of choices that reflect who you are.

**How to Work Through It**

Start by noticing where fear shows up in your body. It might feel like tension in your chest, a knot in your stomach, or a voice in your head that says, "Don't risk it." When you hear that voice, pause. Take a slow breath and remind yourself, "This is fear trying to protect me."

Ask yourself what fear is really afraid of. Sometimes, it's not the situation itself — it's the feeling underneath it. Fear of failure is often fear of shame. Fear of success might actually be fear of change. Fear of love can be fear of being seen. When you name the real source, it becomes smaller.

Next, give yourself permission to feel afraid *and* move anyway. Fear loses its grip when you act in small, safe steps. Try saying what you mean, even if your voice shakes. Try something new without needing it to be perfect. Each time you do, you prove to your body that fear doesn't need to lead.

When fear returns — and it will — treat it like an old guard dog. It barks to warn you, but you get to decide whether there's real danger or just noise.

**What to Remember**

Feeling fear doesn't mean you're weak. It means your body
still believes it has to protect you from the pain of your past.
But you're not that same person anymore. You have more
control, more tools, and more strength than you did back
then.

You don't have to wait for fear to disappear before you move
forward. You just have to remind yourself that it can walk
beside you without steering the way. The goal isn't to live
without fear. It's to live with courage that listens, breathes,
and keeps walking anyway.

# Frustration

**Where You're At**

You feel frustration when life doesn't move the way you want
it to. It's that tight, restless energy that builds up when effort
doesn't equal progress. You try, you wait, you give your best —
and somehow, it's still not enough to make things change.

Frustration can feel like being stuck between doing too much
and being unable to do anything. It's that familiar sense of
wanting to scream into a pillow or walk away from everything
for a while. You're not angry at one thing — you're worn down
by everything.

You might feel impatient with others, with life, or with yourself. You tell yourself to stay calm, but part of you is tired of holding it together. That's not weakness. It's the natural result of carrying effort without reward.

**What's Beneath It**

Feeling frustrated usually comes from having your needs or expectations blocked over and over. Maybe you've poured energy into people who didn't meet you halfway. Maybe you've worked hard toward something that keeps slipping out of reach. Maybe you've been trying to grow, but you keep hitting the same wall inside yourself.

For a lot of people, frustration masks deeper emotions — sadness that things aren't different, fear that change might never come, or exhaustion from always being the one to fix things. When life feels unfair or stuck, frustration steps in to keep you moving. It's your mind's way of saying, "This isn't working, but I don't know what else to do."

**What It Might Look Like**

- You snap easily at people who mean well.

- You feel trapped in patterns that never seem to change.

- You bounce between overworking and giving up.

- You criticize yourself for not being further along.

- You feel restless, tense, or unsatisfied even when things go "right."

## How to Work Through It

Start by naming it. Say, "I feel frustrated." That simple acknowledgment breaks the loop of self-blame. You're not failing — you're feeling.

Then pause and look at what's underneath the tension. Ask yourself, "What did I hope would happen that didn't?" Naming the unmet expectation gives the frustration shape, and once it has shape, it can be addressed.

Next, let some of that energy move through your body. Frustration holds a lot of unused effort — take a walk, clean something, stretch, or breathe deeply until your shoulders loosen. Movement helps release what your mind keeps circling.

Once the edge softens, look at what's still within your control. Focus on the next small, clear step you can take — one thing, not ten. When you take that step, even a tiny one, you remind your brain that you're not powerless.

And sometimes, the most powerful thing you can do is stop pushing. Frustration thrives on force. Clarity comes in stillness. Step back long enough to see whether what you're fighting for is still what you truly want.

## What to Remember

Feeling frustrated doesn't mean you've failed. It means you care — enough to notice when something isn't right, enough to want better.

You don't have to solve everything at once. You just have to pause, breathe, and redirect your energy toward what actually brings peace instead of pressure.

Frustration is the bridge between stuck and change. When you stop fighting it and start listening to it, it becomes a signal — a reminder that your effort deserves direction, not punishment.

# Guilt

### Where You're At

You feel guilt when you believe you've done something wrong, even if all you did was choose yourself. It's that uneasy feeling in your stomach when you say no, take a break, or set a boundary. You worry you've disappointed someone, fallen short, or made things harder for someone else.

Guilt often shows up quietly. It sneaks in after you rest, spend money on yourself, or ask for help. It whispers that you should be doing more, giving more, or caring more. It makes you question whether you're allowed to have needs at all.

Sometimes guilt becomes so familiar that you don't even notice it anymore. It just feels like "being responsible." But underneath that sense of duty is a weight that never lets you rest fully.

## What's Beneath It

Feeling guilt often starts early. Maybe you grew up believing your peace depended on keeping other people happy. Maybe love felt conditional, or mistakes brought disappointment instead of understanding. You learned that being "good" meant avoiding conflict and pleasing others.

That pattern followed you into adulthood. You became the dependable one, the helper, the one who never drops the ball. And when you finally try to do something for yourself, guilt shows up to pull you back in line. It's not that you've done something wrong — it's that your nervous system equates self-care with selfishness.

The truth is that guilt isn't always a moral signal. Sometimes it's a sign that you're growing beyond what was expected of you.

## What It Might Look Like

- You apologize even when you've done nothing wrong.

- You overexplain your decisions because you don't want to be misunderstood.

- You can't relax until everyone else is okay.

- You feel bad for resting when others are still working.

- You replay situations in your head, wondering if you handled them the "right" way.

**How to Work Through It**

Start by asking yourself what your guilt is trying to protect. Often, it's protecting a version of you who learned that peace only came when others were pleased. Thank that part of you for trying to help, then remind it that you're safe to live differently now.

Next, separate guilt from shame. Guilt says, "I did something wrong." Shame says, "I am something wrong." Most of the time, what you're feeling isn't guilt about your actions — it's shame about existing outside of old expectations. You haven't failed anyone by taking care of yourself.

When you feel that familiar pull of guilt, pause before reacting. Breathe. Ask, "Did I actually do something hurtful, or am I just uncomfortable doing something new?" Most guilt fades when you bring logic and compassion into the moment.

If the guilt lingers, talk to it like an old friend. Say, "Thank you for keeping me kind and aware. But I'm allowed to be kind to myself, too." Then move forward anyway. The more often you do that, the quieter guilt becomes.

**What to Remember**

Feeling guilt doesn't mean you've done something wrong. It often means you're doing something different — something that honors your limits, your truth, or your peace.

You don't have to apologize for being human. You don't have to earn your rest, your joy, or your needs. Let guilt be a teacher, not a jailer. Learn from what it shows you, then let it go.

You can be thoughtful without overthinking, generous without overgiving, and caring without carrying everything. Guilt loses its grip the moment you realize you were never meant to hold the world together — only yourself.

# Hopelessness

### Where You're At

You feel hopeless when it seems like nothing will ever get better. It's that heavy sense of "what's the point?" when every effort feels wasted, every step forward slides you back, and the light you've been walking toward seems to fade no matter how far you go.

Hopelessness isn't loud. It's quiet and heavy. It shows up when you're too tired to care, when even hope itself feels like a burden. You might still get up, still go to work, still smile when people ask how you are — but inside, you feel detached from the future, like you've stopped expecting good things to happen.

Sometimes it doesn't even feel like sadness anymore. It's just emptiness, a dull ache that makes you wonder if you'll ever feel inspired, loved, or alive again.

## What's Beneath It

Feeling hopeless is often what happens after trying too hard for too long without relief. It can come from disappointment, loss, trauma, or burnout. When your nervous system stays in survival mode for months or years, hope starts to feel unrealistic — even dangerous. You stop hoping to protect yourself from the pain of being let down again.

Maybe you've been strong for so long that exhaustion looks like failure. Maybe you've carried responsibilities that never seem to lighten. Maybe you've believed things would change, but they didn't — at least not yet.

Hopelessness doesn't mean you've given up. It means your heart is begging for rest.

## What It Might Look Like

- You go through the motions but feel detached from everything.

- You find it hard to get excited about plans or goals.

- You feel like your effort doesn't matter or won't change anything.

- You isolate because you don't want to drain others with how you feel.

- You tell yourself you don't care, but deep down you wish you still did.

**How to Work Through It**

Start by removing the pressure to "stay positive." You don't need to force optimism. You just need to make space for honesty. Say to yourself, "I feel hopeless right now." That's not weakness — that's truth. And truth is often the first step back to strength.

Then, shrink your focus. Hopelessness grows when your mind looks too far ahead. Bring your attention to what's right in front of you — the next breath, the next meal, the next small task. You don't have to solve your whole life today. You just have to make it through this moment.

Reach for something that reminds you of life, even if it's small. Step outside. Feel the air. Listen to music. Watch light move through a window. These small acts aren't pointless — they're proof that life is still happening, even when you feel disconnected from it.

If you can, talk to someone. Hopelessness thrives in isolation. Sharing what feels heavy doesn't fix it instantly, but it lightens the load. Let someone witness what you're feeling. You don't need advice — just presence.

And if you can't find hope for yourself right now, borrow someone else's. Believe the people who remind you that you've made it through before, even if you can't feel it yet.

**What to Remember**

Feeling hopeless doesn't mean you're broken. It means you've reached the limit of carrying things alone.

You don't have to force hope — you just have to stay open to it returning. It always does, quietly and slowly, in moments that remind you life hasn't forgotten you.

There's nothing weak about being tired. You've survived every day you thought you couldn't, and that's not failure — that's proof. Even when it doesn't feel like it, hope is still alive somewhere inside you, waiting for the space to breathe again.

# Insecurity

**Where You're At**

You feel insecurity when you start to doubt your value, your place, or your ability to measure up. It's that uneasy feeling that other people have something you don't — more confidence, more charm, more belonging. You question how you come across, how you're being seen, or whether you're enough for the moment you're in.

Sometimes insecurity whispers quietly. Other times, it shouts. You replay your words after a conversation, overthink how people respond, or look at your reflection and focus only on what you'd change. You might even avoid opportunities because you fear being exposed as unqualified or undeserving.

Insecurity makes you look for evidence that you're falling short — and you'll always find it if that's what you're searching for.

**What's Beneath It**

Feeling insecure usually starts when love, praise, or approval were tied to performance. Maybe you learned early that being good enough meant being perfect, achieving more, or staying out of trouble. When acceptance depends on effort, you grow into an adult who's always chasing proof that you matter.

Insecurity can also come from comparison. You see people who seem effortless or confident and assume they're built differently. But confidence isn't a gift — it's a practice. Everyone you admire has doubted themselves, too.

At its core, insecurity isn't about vanity. It's about safety — the need to know you're accepted even when you're not performing.

**What It Might Look Like**

- You second-guess your decisions or ask for constant reassurance.

- You downplay compliments or dismiss your own achievements.

- You compare your progress to others and feel behind.

- You struggle to speak up or share ideas for fear of being judged.

- You work extra hard to seem confident, even when you don't feel it.

**How to Work Through It**

Start by catching your self-talk. Notice the words you use when you think about yourself. Would you say those same things to someone you love? If not, they don't belong to you. Replace judgment with curiosity. Instead of asking, "What's wrong with me?" try asking, "What part of me still needs reassurance?"

Remind yourself that confidence isn't the absence of doubt — it's the decision to keep showing up even when you feel unsure. You don't have to wait until you feel ready to act. Action builds confidence faster than thinking ever will.

Limit comparison by grounding yourself in reality. What you see in others is a highlight, not the whole picture. The parts of yourself you criticize are often the same parts others find most relatable.

If insecurity is tied to specific experiences — rejection, criticism, or failure — revisit those memories with compassion. Tell your younger self what they needed to hear then: "You did your best. You were worthy even before you proved anything."

And when insecurity shows up again, don't panic. It's just your mind asking for reassurance. Give it gently. You can remind yourself, "I've felt this before, and I've handled it before." That's how you retrain your brain to see yourself as safe and capable.

**What to Remember**

Feeling insecure doesn't mean you're weak. It means you're human enough to want connection and honest enough to admit you care how you're seen.

You don't have to be perfect to be worthy. You don't have to feel confident to show up. You just have to stop waiting for certainty before believing in yourself.

Confidence isn't found in what others say about you. It's built quietly, each time you keep a promise to yourself, each time you show up as you are. That's how you turn insecurity into trust — not trust in the world, but trust in you.

# Jealousy

**Where You're At**

You feel jealousy when you see someone with something you deeply want — attention, success, love, freedom, confidence — and it stirs something uncomfortable inside you. You don't want to feel it. You might even feel ashamed of it. But still, it lingers. It makes you compare, question, and sometimes withdraw.

Jealousy isn't about wishing harm on anyone. It's about the ache of not having what you believe would finally make you feel enough. You might scroll through social media, watch someone's life unfold, and feel a mix of admiration and pain. You tell yourself to be happy for them — and you are — but you're also asking quietly, "Why not me?"

That question doesn't make you selfish. It makes you honest.

**What's Beneath It**

Feeling jealous often comes from the belief that good things are scarce — that there's only so much love, attention, or opportunity to go around. Maybe you grew up having to compete for what should have been freely given. Maybe praise or affection were rare, so when someone else gets it, it stings.

Sometimes jealousy points to the parts of yourself you've been neglecting. When you see someone living with confidence, peace, or purpose, what you're really seeing is a reflection of something in you that's longing to wake up.

Jealousy isn't a moral flaw. It's a compass, quietly showing you where you've been starving for something that matters.

**What It Might Look Like**

- You compare your life or progress to others and always come up short.

- You downplay someone else's success to feel less behind.

- You overwork to prove you deserve what they have.

- You avoid people who trigger insecurity, even if you care about them.

- You feel distant from your own gratitude because comparison keeps you focused on lack.

**How to Work Through It**

Start by admitting it. "I feel jealous." Saying it doesn't make you petty — it makes you aware. You can't heal what you won't name.

Then, instead of turning that energy outward, turn it inward. Ask, "What does their life or situation awaken in me?" Is it freedom, love, recognition, rest? Usually, jealousy reveals something you already value — something you've told yourself you can't have.

Next, remind yourself that someone else's abundance doesn't mean there's less for you. Life isn't a race; it's a mirror. What you see in others is evidence of what's possible, not proof of your failure.

Take that longing seriously. If you envy someone's peace, it might be time to slow down. If you envy their courage, it might be time to take a small risk. Jealousy loses power when you use it as information instead of ammunition.

Finally, practice gratitude — not as a guilt trip, but as grounding. Look at what's already in your life that once felt out of reach. Gratitude doesn't erase desire; it balances it with perspective.

**What to Remember**

Feeling jealous doesn't mean you're unkind or shallow. It means you're aware of something beautiful that you want more of in your own life.

You don't have to judge that feeling. You just have to listen to it. Let it show you what's missing, what matters, and what's next.

Jealousy doesn't point to what you lack — it points to what's waiting to grow. When you shift from comparison to curiosity, you turn envy into inspiration. And that's how you move from longing to living.

# Loneliness

**Where You're At**

You feel lonely when you crave connection but can't seem to reach it. You might be surrounded by people and still feel unseen. You might have friends, a family, or a partner, but deep down you feel misunderstood — like no one really *gets* you.

Loneliness doesn't always mean being alone. It often means feeling invisible. You smile, talk, work, and show up, but part of you is still waiting for someone to notice how much you wish you could let your guard down.

It can make you question your worth. You might wonder if you're hard to love, too different, or simply not enough. But loneliness isn't proof that you're broken — it's proof that you were made for deeper connection than you've been getting.

**What's Beneath It**

Feeling lonely often comes from growing up in spaces where emotional presence was missing. Maybe the people around you provided for you, but they didn't really *see* you. Maybe love was shown through actions, not words. Maybe you learned that expressing your feelings pushed people away instead of pulling them closer.

So you learned to shrink your needs, to stay surface-level, to play the role people wanted from you. That protected you, but it also kept you from being truly known. The loneliness you feel now isn't just about who's around you — it's about how safe you feel to be yourself when they are.

**What It Might Look Like**

- You spend time with people but leave feeling drained or unseen.

- You downplay what's bothering you because you don't think anyone will understand.

- You isolate when you need connection the most.

- You look confident on the outside but feel empty inside.

- You crave closeness but feel uncomfortable when you get it.

**How to Work Through It** Start by telling yourself the truth — you want connection. That doesn't make you needy. It makes you human. Wanting to be known isn't weakness; it's the foundation of real belonging.

Then, look at the kind of connection you've been settling for. Sometimes, loneliness lingers because you're surrounded by people who can't meet you where you are. It's okay to want more depth. It's okay to outgrow shallow relationships.

Begin with small honesty. When someone asks how you are, answer a little more truthfully than usual. When you feel hurt, name it instead of hiding it. Real connection only happens when someone can see what's actually true about you.

If you don't have people in your life who can meet you in that space right now, start by showing up for yourself. Write down what you wish someone would say to you. Say it to yourself. Go outside, call someone you trust, or spend time doing something that brings you peace. Loneliness shrinks in moments of truth — even if you're the one providing it.

**What to Remember**

Feeling lonely doesn't mean you're unlovable. It means you're disconnected — from others, yes, but also from your own emotional truth.

You can build new kinds of relationships, but first, you have to show up as the real you. The right people can't find you if you keep hiding behind the version of yourself that never needs anything.

You don't need to wait to be chosen to belong. You belong the moment you decide to stop hiding. Loneliness fades when you remember that being known starts with being honest — with yourself first, and then with the world.

# Numbness

**Where You're At**

You feel numb when life stops registering. You go through the motions — work, talk, smile, help — but everything feels muted, like you're watching your own life from a distance. You can't tell if you're tired, sad, or just over it. You know you should care, but you can't seem to make yourself feel anything at all.

Numbness can feel like nothing and everything at the same time. It's the quiet after too much noise, the stillness after too many storms. You might miss feeling alive, but you're also afraid that if you start to feel again, it'll all come rushing in at once.

You're not broken for feeling numb. Your body just decided that silence was safer than the noise of your emotions.

**What's Beneath It**

Feeling numb is usually the body's way of saying, "That's enough for now." When you've been carrying too much pain, stress, or responsibility for too long, your nervous system starts to shut down emotion to keep you functioning. It's not a failure of feeling — it's a defense mechanism.

Maybe you grew up in a place where expressing emotions wasn't allowed or wasn't safe. Maybe life taught you that if you showed too much, it would only make things worse. So your body learned to turn the volume down on emotion altogether. It's a skill that once helped you survive, but now it keeps you from experiencing joy, excitement, and connection too.

Numbness isn't the absence of emotion — it's the body's pause button.

**What It Might Look Like**

- You can't remember the last time you felt truly excited or inspired.

- You disconnect in conversations or zone out easily.

- You use distractions — scrolling, eating, drinking, or overworking — to fill the silence.

- You feel calm on the surface but empty underneath.

- You have moments of guilt for not feeling grateful or happy enough.

**How to Work Through It**

Start small. You don't need to force yourself to "feel more." You need to gently remind your body that it's safe to feel again. The best way to do that is through presence, not pressure.

Move your body slowly — walk, stretch, breathe deeply. Physical movement sends signals of safety to your brain. Pay attention to your senses. What can you see, smell, hear, and touch right now? Feeling starts by noticing the smallest things.

If numbness has lasted a long time, it might feel like nothing works at first. That's okay. Stay patient. The goal isn't to force emotion back in — it's to create space for it to return naturally.

Try writing or talking about what used to bring you joy. Look through old photos, listen to music that stirs something, or visit a place that once felt meaningful. These are gentle ways of reminding your body that life still holds warmth, even if you can't feel it yet.

And when the feelings start to come back — even the hard ones — let them. Feeling sad or angry after being numb isn't a setback. It's progress. It means the walls are starting to lower.

**What to Remember**

Feeling numb doesn't mean you don't care. It means you've cared too much for too long without enough rest or relief.

You don't need to rush this process. Your emotions are waiting for safety, not effort. They'll return when your body believes it's okay to feel again.

You haven't lost your capacity to feel — you've just paused it. When you treat yourself with patience and gentleness, the color starts to come back. Life doesn't rush healing, and neither should you.

# Overwhelm

**Where You're At**

You feel overwhelmed when life feels too loud, too fast, or too heavy to keep up with. It's that moment when you can't think straight because everything feels urgent and your mind won't stop listing what's next. You might feel like you're constantly behind, even when you've done everything you can.

Overwhelm often hits after a long stretch of holding it all together. You wake up tired. You can't focus. Small decisions suddenly feel impossible. Sometimes you cry over something simple, not because it's big, but because it's the thing that finally tipped the scale.

You might tell yourself you just need to try harder. But you're not lazy or weak. You're simply overloaded.

**What's Beneath It**

Feeling overwhelmed is what happens when your mind and body have been in survival mode for too long without rest. It's not just about having too much to do — it's about carrying more than any one person should have to carry alone.

For a lot of people, overwhelm starts in childhood. Maybe you learned to take responsibility early. Maybe you were the one who kept peace, helped others, or stayed calm when everything else was falling apart. You didn't have time to feel, so you learned to keep moving. Now, as an adult, that same instinct runs your life. You power through exhaustion because slowing down feels like failure.

Overwhelm isn't about weakness. It's what happens when strength isn't allowed to rest.

**What It Might Look Like**

- You jump from task to task but never feel caught up.

- You forget things easily because your brain is juggling too much.

- You feel irritable or shut down emotionally when people ask for more.

- You cancel plans or isolate, not because you don't care, but because you're spent.

- You scroll, snack, or zone out just to escape the noise in your mind.

**How to Work Through It**

The first step is to slow everything down — not just your body, but your mind. Take one deep breath and remind yourself that not everything is urgent. Some things can wait. You don't have to earn rest.

Then, focus on one small thing you can do right now. Pick something simple and complete it. Overwhelm grows when you try to do everything at once. It shrinks when you focus on one thing fully. When that's done, take another breath before moving to the next.

Give yourself permission to pause. Walk outside. Step away from your phone. Let your nervous system catch up to your body. You don't have to solve your whole life this hour. You just have to create a little bit of space.

When you feel that tightness in your chest or that urge to shut down, ask yourself: "What's one thing I can put down right now?" Maybe it's a task. Maybe it's a worry. Maybe it's someone else's expectation.

Rest isn't avoidance. It's maintenance. When you take breaks, you're not quitting — you're resetting your system so you can handle life from a place of clarity, not chaos.

**What to Remember**

Feeling overwhelmed doesn't mean you're failing. It means you've been carrying too much for too long. It's okay to stop. It's okay to let something go. The world will keep spinning even when you take a breath.

You are allowed to rest before you break. You don't have to prove your worth by surviving exhaustion. You've done enough. The next right thing might simply be to sit still, breathe, and remember that you are human — and that's enough for today.

# Rejection

**Where You're At**

You feel rejection when something or someone tells you no —
when you reach out, show up, or take a risk, and it isn't
returned. It can sting like a physical wound. Maybe it was a
job you didn't get, a person who pulled away, or a friend who
didn't choose you back. Even when you tell yourself it's not a
big deal, it still lingers.

Rejection makes you question your worth. It leaves you
wondering what was wrong with you, what you could've done
differently, or why you weren't enough this time. You might
brush it off in public but feel it deeply in private. And when it
happens more than once, it starts to shape how you see
yourself.

You don't just fear being rejected again — you start to protect
yourself from it by never fully trying.

**What's Beneath It**

Feeling rejected touches one of the deepest human fears —
the fear of disconnection. We're wired to need belonging, to
want to be accepted and valued. When that bond breaks, even
in small ways, it hits the part of your brain that registers
pain.

If you've experienced rejection early in life — through
neglect, criticism, or conditional love — it can leave a lasting
mark. You might start believing you have to perform, please,
or achieve to be wanted. So every "no" feels like proof that the

old story was right — that you're too much, not enough, or just not the right kind of person to be chosen.

But rejection says far less about your worth than it does about someone else's capacity. Sometimes people can't see you fully because they're still learning to see themselves.

**What It Might Look Like**

- You replay what went wrong, looking for clues or closure.

- You take small rejections — being ignored, overlooked, or misunderstood — personally.

- You hesitate to open up or take risks again.

- You downplay your wants to avoid being told no.

- You compare yourself to others and wonder what they have that you don't.

**How to Work Through It**

Start by acknowledging the hurt. Rejection isn't something to "get over." It's something to process. Say to yourself, "That hurt because I cared." Let that truth stand without trying to minimize it.

Then, separate the event from your identity. You weren't rejected because you're unworthy; you were rejected because something didn't align. Sometimes rejection is protection — closing one door so another can open that actually fits you.

Remind yourself that rejection is part of connection. Every person who's ever been loved has also been rejected. Every person who's found their place had to face the places they didn't belong first. It's not a reflection of failure — it's the sorting process of life.

If rejection still stings, write down what it brought up for you. Did it tap into an old wound? A memory of being left out or overlooked? Sometimes what hurts most isn't the moment itself but what it reminds you of. Seeing that clearly helps you respond to *this* moment instead of reliving the old one.

**What to Remember**

Feeling rejection doesn't mean you're not good enough. It means you reached for something real — connection, opportunity, belonging. That's brave.

You're not defined by who didn't choose you. You're shaped by how you choose yourself afterward.

Rejection is painful, yes, but it's also revealing. It shows you what you value, what you long for, and what kind of love or space you're meant to hold out for. The next time it happens, remember — the right doors don't close. They open easily, without convincing, when they're truly meant for you.

# Resentment

## Where You're At

You feel resentment when you've given more than you've received. It builds quietly, one small disappointment at a time. You tell yourself you're fine, that you're being kind, patient, or understanding — but somewhere deep down, you're tired of always being the one who bends.

Resentment isn't always obvious. It can sound polite. It hides behind phrases like "It's no big deal" or "I don't mind." You say those words to keep peace, but inside, you're keeping score. Not because you want to, but because no one seems to notice how much you give.

Resentment grows in silence. It starts as self-protection, but over time, it turns connection into obligation.

## What's Beneath It

Feeling resentment usually means your boundaries have been crossed too many times without acknowledgment. You've learned to meet everyone else's needs while ignoring your own. Maybe you were raised to believe that being helpful made you good, and that asking for anything in return was selfish. So you kept giving, even when it hurt.

The truth is, resentment is a mix of anger and sadness — anger that you've been taken for granted, and sadness that you didn't know how to stop it. It isn't about bitterness. It's about imbalance.

Resentment often hides a deeper message: "I'm exhausted from pretending this doesn't bother me."

**What It Might Look Like**

- You feel irritated by people you also love deeply.

- You start avoiding people or tasks that once mattered to you.

- You agree to help, then feel drained or bitter afterward.

- You replay old situations, thinking about what you should have said.

- You struggle to celebrate others because you feel unseen yourself.

**How to Work Through It**

The first step is to admit the truth — that you're tired. You don't have to justify it or make it sound noble. You can love people and still feel resentful toward them. Both can be true.

Next, ask yourself what boundary was crossed. What did you need that you didn't ask for? What did you keep saying yes to when your body was saying no? Resentment is a map pointing back to your neglected needs.

Once you see where it started, give yourself permission to change the pattern. That might mean saying no without explaining. It might mean asking for help before you hit your limit. It might mean doing less out of guilt and more out of choice.

It's okay if that feels uncomfortable at first. You've trained people to expect you to give endlessly. Changing that dynamic might disappoint them, but it will set you free.

If the resentment feels too heavy to release, try writing it down. Be honest. No one else needs to read it. Seeing your feelings in words helps you separate what's still real from what's simply built up. Then take a breath and decide what you'll no longer carry.

**What to Remember**

Feeling resentment doesn't make you ungrateful or unkind. It means your kindness has gone unreturned for too long. You don't have to harden to protect yourself. You just have to start honoring your own limits.

Resentment is a signal, not a sentence. It's your heart saying, "I've given enough in silence." The moment you start listening to that voice, you stop waiting for others to change and start reclaiming your peace.

# Sadness

## Where You're At

You feel sadness when something meaningful is missing, lost, or changing. It's the heaviness that settles in your chest when you realize things didn't turn out how you hoped. It can come from heartbreak, grief, disappointment, or even quiet moments when life feels still but empty.

Sometimes sadness is obvious — tears, loss, endings. But other times, it hides under irritability, tiredness, or numbness. You might say you're "fine," but deep down, you know something is off. You feel slower, quieter, less connected to the things that used to bring joy.

You may not want to call it sadness because sadness feels weak. But the truth is, sadness is what allows you to grieve the gap between what you wanted and what you have. It's not a flaw. It's a signal that you've cared deeply about something.

## What's Beneath It

Feeling sadness usually means you're in touch with something real. Many of us learned early on to hide sadness because it made others uncomfortable. Maybe you were told to cheer up, toughen up, or stop crying. Maybe you learned that emotions made people pull away instead of come closer.

So you learned to swallow sadness instead of feel it. But unspoken sadness doesn't disappear — it turns into fatigue, irritability, or emptiness. When you don't allow sadness, your body still carries the weight of what was never mourned.

Sadness is your body's way of slowing you down long enough to process what your mind hasn't caught up to yet.

**What It Might Look Like**

- You feel detached from things you used to care about.

- You cry easily or not at all, but either way, you feel heavy.

- You replay memories that bring both comfort and pain.

- You struggle to find motivation, even for things you enjoy.

- You distract yourself to avoid being alone with your thoughts.

**How to Work Through It**

The only way through sadness is to let yourself feel it. Not all at once, not dramatically — just honestly. Sit with it. Cry if you need to. Write if you can't find words to say out loud. There is no prize for holding it in.

Let yourself grieve what was lost — the person, the plan, the version of life you imagined. Grief isn't self-pity. It's love with nowhere to go. The more you allow yourself to acknowledge what hurts, the lighter your heart becomes.

Move your body gently. Go for a walk. Sit in sunlight. Listen to music that matches how you feel instead of fighting it. Sadness doesn't need to be fixed. It needs to be witnessed.

If the sadness lingers, remind yourself it's not permanent. Feelings are visitors, not residents. This one will pass too — not because you force it to, but because you've honored its purpose.

**What to Remember**

Feeling sadness doesn't mean you're broken. It means you've cared. It means your heart still works.

You don't have to rush to be happy again. Healing isn't about erasing the sadness. It's about making space for joy to return when it's ready.

You can hold sadness and still be whole. Let it do its work. Let it soften what's hard and remind you that even in loss, you're still alive — and that's something sacred.

# Self-Blame

**Where You're At**

You feel self-blame when something goes wrong and your first thought is, "This is my fault." You replay what happened, searching for every place you could have done better, said more, or seen it coming. Even when logic tells you it wasn't all on you, the guilt lingers.

You might think you're being responsible, but what's really happening is that you're trying to control pain. If it's your fault, then maybe you can fix it. Maybe you can keep it from happening again. But that same instinct that once made you careful now makes you cruel to yourself.

You can forgive others easily, but when it comes to you, grace feels out of reach.

## What's Beneath It

Feeling self-blame often comes from growing up in environments where peace depended on you. Maybe you were the one who smoothed things over, who stayed quiet to avoid conflict, or who carried the blame to keep others calm. You learned that being at fault was safer than being at odds.

As an adult, that pattern continues. When something breaks, you rush to take ownership. When relationships fail, you look inward first. It's not because you're self-aware — it's because you learned that safety came from fixing, not feeling.

But not everything that hurts is yours to carry. Self-blame turns natural empathy into self-punishment.

## What It Might Look Like

- You replay conversations, wondering what you could've done differently.

- You take on responsibility for other people's emotions.

- You feel guilty for resting, saying no, or putting yourself first.

- You apologize even when you didn't do anything wrong.

- You struggle to let go of mistakes, no matter how small.

**How to Work Through It**

Start by separating responsibility from control. You can be responsible *for yourself* without being responsible *for everything*. Ask, "What part of this is truly mine, and what part isn't?" Write it down if it helps. Seeing it clearly makes it harder to carry what doesn't belong to you.

Then, practice talking to yourself the way you'd talk to a friend. If someone you loved made the same mistake, would you speak to them the way you speak to yourself? Probably not. That gap between how you treat others and how you treat yourself is where healing begins.

When the urge to self-blame appears, pause before reacting. Instead of asking, "What did I do wrong?" try, "What can I learn from this without shaming myself?" Growth doesn't require guilt. It requires honesty and compassion.

If forgiveness feels too far away, start smaller. Begin with permission. Permission to be human. Permission to have limits. Permission to be learning.

**What to Remember**

Feeling self-blame doesn't make you responsible for everything that's gone wrong. It means you've carried too much accountability for too long.

You don't have to earn peace by punishing yourself. You don't have to fix everything to deserve rest.

The world doesn't get lighter because you take on more. It gets lighter when you finally set down what was never yours.

# Shame

**Where You're At**

You feel shame when something inside you whispers that you're not enough. It's more than embarrassment or regret — it's that deep, heavy feeling that something about you is wrong. You might not say it out loud, but it shows up as an urge to hide, to shrink, or to pretend you're fine when you're not.

Shame can sneak in when you make a mistake, when someone criticizes you, or even when you succeed. It tells you that if people really saw you — all of you — they might turn away. So you try harder, smile wider, and stay busy enough to never have to feel it. But underneath the surface, you're carrying a quiet fear: "What if I'm not lovable as I am?"

## What's Beneath It

Feeling shame usually starts when your sense of worth becomes tied to performance, approval, or perfection. Maybe love or attention came when you did well, stayed quiet, or kept things together. Maybe being vulnerable once led to being laughed at, rejected, or punished.

Those moments teach your nervous system a painful rule — that being yourself isn't safe. So you build a version of you that feels more acceptable. You become polished, helpful, put-together. You earn your place instead of simply taking up space.

But shame isn't the truth about who you are. It's a learned reaction that formed to keep you from being hurt again.

## What It Might Look Like

- You replay old mistakes in your head and still feel embarrassed or small.

- You struggle to accept compliments or deflect them quickly.

- You overachieve or overgive to prove your worth.

- You feel uncomfortable asking for help or showing emotion.

- You feel exposed when someone gets too close, even in kindness.

**How to Work Through It**

The first step to softening shame is to bring it into the light. Shame grows in secrecy. The moment you name it, it loses power. Say to yourself, "I feel shame right now." Notice where it sits in your body. Maybe it feels like heat in your face, pressure in your chest, or tension in your stomach.

Then remind yourself that this feeling doesn't define you. You are not shame — you're experiencing it. That difference matters. When you stop identifying with the feeling, you create room to observe it without drowning in it.

Next, bring compassion to the part of you that feels small. Ask, "What is this part of me afraid will happen if I'm seen?" Most of the time, the answer is rejection. The fear is that you'll lose connection if you're real. But connection built on pretending isn't real connection at all.

When shame tries to convince you to hide, practice doing the opposite. Share something small and honest with someone safe. Write down what you wish you could say. Sit with the discomfort instead of running from it. Each time you stay present through the feeling, you teach your body that being authentic isn't dangerous.

## What to Remember

Feeling shame doesn't mean you're broken. It means you were made to feel unsafe for being yourself — but that story isn't yours to keep.

You are not a mistake. You are a human being learning to unlearn old survival patterns. The parts of you that you hide are often the ones most worthy of love.

You don't heal shame by proving your worth. You heal it by remembering you never had to earn it in the first place.

www.ingramcontent.com/pod-product-compliance
Lightning Source LLC
Chambersburg PA
CBHW071220090426
42736CB00014B/2913